MW01109738

LIVING AT YOUR VERY BEST

I'M DOING BETTER

NATE HOLCOMB

HIM
PUBLISHING

I'm Doing Better
By Nate Holcomb

Copyright © 2019
Nate Holcomb

ISBN: 978-1-930918-65-8

Printed in the United States of America

Him Publishing
P.O. Box 960
Copperas Cove, TX 76522
www.HimPublishing.com

Him Publishing, Inc. is a ministry of
The Cathedral of Central Texas,
CHRISTIAN HOUSE OF PRAYER MINISTRIES, INC.
www.chop.org

Nate Holcomb
will always be remembered
and never forgotten.
When we think of him,
we can hear his voice saying,
"I'm Doing Better because
I'm in the Best Place.".

TABLE OF CONTENTS

INTRODUCTION

GOOD, BETTER, BEST . . . never let it rest until your good is better and your better is best. This phrase is as applicable today as it was when it was coined back in 347 A.D., by St. Jerome, author of The Vulgate.

The drive in its cadence still underscores the need to progress, to move forward, to continuously improve. It emphasizes that doing better isn't a mediocre undertaking but requires initiative and a committed pursuit.

Doing better is not a stagnant nor sedentary process; it is progressive. It is constant growth. It's the 30, 60, and 100-fold concept of fruit-bearing (Mark 4:20). It's "first the blade, then the ear, after that the full corn in the ear" type of progression (Mark 4:28).

To do better requires a forward reaching mind-set that, in degrees and stages, ultimately leads to prosperity. For in order to prosper, you must learn to do better.

Prosperity and doing better are actually synonymous terms. In fact, many African tribes translate the term prosper as 'doing better.'

Whether rich or poor, young or old, everyone wants to do better. Therefore, each of us must come to an understanding that to do better is always possible. No matter who you are, regardless of your status in life, doing better is achievable and it is God's will for you.

The desire to do better originates with God, whose loving-kindness is better than life (Psalm 63:3). Consider that after the Old Covenant, He gave us a better covenant, established on better promises (Hebrews 8:6). He wants us to understand He's not withholding anything that would benefit or give us the advantage. Indeed, it is His good pleasure to give us the kingdom.

The enemy's goal is quite the opposite. He seeks to steal, to kill, and to destroy (John 10:10). Rather than progress, he wants you to regress. He aspires to halt your forward momentum and drive you backwards, robbing you of what you had in the first place.

The woman with the issue of blood was no stranger to his larceny. The Scripture says she had suffered many things of many physicians. Spending all that she had, she was nothing bettered, but rather grew worse (Mark 5:25-26).

Worse is better's antonym. The fact that she grew worse speaks of her incremental decline. It tells us that throughout this 12 year ordeal, she was not advantaged in any way. Rather, she suffered painfully at the hands of people who were supposed to heal her, to make her better. Those supposedly skilled in the art of healing, had made her worse and charged her for it. She had exhausted her finances on their remedies but was worsened by them. Trying to get better, she became worse.

Even so, the woman refused to give up. Determined to get better, she kept pressing forward until she found the true source of her betterment—Jesus. When she touched the tassel on the edge of His garment, she immediately got better (Mark 5:28).

The unnamed woman encapsulates the Everyman concept. She represents ordinary individuals who can easily identify with her plight. Your situation might not be due to health; perhaps divorce has placed you in reduced circumstances. Whatever the cause, a vital lesson can be gleaned from this woman's experience and it is this: she did not misconstrue man's inability to help her as the be-all and end-all of her doing better. No. She took the matter out of the hands of man and put it in the hands of God. It wasn't until she touched Jesus that she got better; and no marvel, for ". . .beyond all contradiction the lesser is blessed by the better" (Hebrews 7:7 NKJV).

III John 1:2 says, "Beloved, I wish above all things that thou mayest prosper and be in health, even as thy soul prospereth." This verse tells us that God desires for us to prosper or in other words, to do better. Since it is His will, then whatever the circumstances, it is a setup to give you the advantage.

Remember, when you're down to nothing, God is up to something and it's always for you to live at your very best.

Therefore if any man

be in Christ, he is a new

creature: old things are

passed away; behold, all

things are become new.

2ND CORINTHIANS 5:17

YOU DON'T HAVE TO LOSE YOUR MIND

OUR WORLD IS IN BAD SHAPE. This statement does not come from a place of negativity. I'm not given to bouts of depression nor am I prone to pessimism. The shape of the world sets the stage for what we need the most—help.

The Lord is our helper. He will provide protection, but in most cases there will be no prevention. Bad things happen to all people. No one is exempt from pain, pressure or problems. However, when negative circumstances occur we can use them toward our development or allow them to bring our detriment. Understand, choosing development over detriment brings us into the right mind-set.

Our outcome depends on our state of mind. The human mind is the battleground where spiritual warfare takes place. Where is your mind right now? Are you bombarded with bad news or are you mentally positioned in a place of peace? The answer to this question relies on the choices you make. Listen, your position with Jesus Christ must supersede your condition in life.

Declare today, "I'm doing better!" This declaration must take you beyond a mental ascent; it needs to establish a lifestyle. Remember, what you believe will determine how you behave. Therefore, if you believe you're doing better, you'll act better and eventually be better.

We can lose just about anything in this world and recover from the loss, but we never want to lose our minds. Losing one's mind is the gateway to an unproductive life. Jesus came to give us a fruitful life. However, the devil tries to counteract the Lord's plan by filling our lives with misfortune at every turn. Even still, we have a choice. We can choose to focus on the misfortunes or follow the admonition of the apostle Paul in Romans 12.

MOVING FROM CONFORMING

And be not conformed to this world: *but be ye transformed by the renewing of your mind, that ye may prove what is that good, and acceptable, and perfect, will of God. (Romans 12:2 Bold Added)*

Every day we have to choose to live above the common fray of this world's negativity, poverty, hypocrisy and the gravity that tries to pull us down. This is the attitude that Paul chose.

The apostle Paul wrote a profound and most encouraging letter to a church he established in the region of Philippi. He instructed the church to remain optimistic despite the troubles they were facing. Now, what made his letter so remarkable is the fact that Paul himself was undergoing tragic circumstances.

He had been arrested for teaching the gospel of Jesus Christ. Paul was transported from one trial to another and his final destination was the highest court in Rome. He was accused of treason and if convicted, he would face execution. Nevertheless, Paul admonished the Philippian church to rejoice in the Lord always.

Before finding himself wrapped in court proceedings and dire predicaments Paul was a man of impeccable pedigree. He spoke several languages. His contemporaries wrote the laws for the commoners to follow. His religious résumé met the approval of the most esteemed synagogue scholars. You could say Paul was conformed to the world that surrounded him. In fact, he allowed his pedigree to swell his ego.

Pride causes some people to think of themselves in grandiose fashions. The things they acquire make them feel they're better than less fortunate people. We have to be careful not to allow possessions or positions to create an arrogant mindset. This becomes another way of losing our minds and ultimately ourselves.

While riding to Damascus, Paul was knocked off his high-horse. We can say the Lord brought him down to earth. Paul's conformity to the rituals of men prohibited him from seeing God clearly. Therefore, the Lord took his eyesight. However, through the loss of his natural eyesight, he gained spiritual insight.

Losses are a part of life. We can learn a lot about an individual just by observing their response to a loss. Our losses can become a source of pain or a point of circumspection. Some people can't live without some things. Their entire life crumbles when facing forfeiture. Now, I am not minimizing losing things. Respectfully, some defeats can seem overwhelming such as losing a business, home, health or even a dear loved one. Although these losses can deliver a devastating blow, we don't have to lose our mind. Through loses we should learn there is still something to gain.

God wants us to develop the mind-set that if we lose everything we hold dear, but still have Him; we have enough to start again. This world measures success by the things we possess. Yet, we are not to conform to this world. Taking a loss doesn't mean we stop living, it demands we start learning. In a crisis we will either *lose* the faith we have in God or *learn* more about the God we place our faith in. So, choose not to lose, but to learn.

Upon losing his eyesight, Paul gained insight. He was able to hear from God unlike when he had his vision. The Lord showed Paul his destiny and gave him direction.

Perhaps you need God to reveal your destiny. If you're loss and need direction seek the Lord. Conforming to this world causes you to become so distracted and you fail to have time for God. Jesus said it's possible to gain the world and lose your soul. A major element of the soul is the mind. Don't conform to having passions for the things of this world, set your passion on the Lord.

The adage "You win some, you lose some" holds a lot of truth. We all experience good and bad days. We will not always be dealt a winning hand, but it doesn't mean we're losers. Let's play the hand we're given and if we lose the hand, we can smile and determine not to lose our minds.

Every day brings the possibilities of doing better. Begin taking advantage of each new day. Make the decision to move away from being conformed to being transformed.

MOTIVATED BY TRANSFORMING

And be not conformed to this world: **but be ye transformed by the renewing of your mind**, *that ye may prove what is that good, and acceptable, and perfect, will of God. (Romans 12:2 Bold Added)*

The process of transformation starts with us renewing our minds. This world presents many challenges. The difficulties of life can cause us to worry. However, the Lord wants us to renew our mind from a state of anxiety to a place of peace.

The way we maintain peace of mind is by being careful for

nothing. There are times when I depart from a person's presence and the individual says, "Take care." I'm aware this is another way of saying, "Good bye." However, I have learned words have power. Therefore, I refuse to take care, but rather I choose to give them to the Lord. After all, He can handle my cares much better than I can.

> *Be careful for nothing; but in every thing by*
> *prayer and supplication with thanksgiving*
> *let your requests be made known unto God.*
> *And the peace of God, which passeth all*
> *understanding, shall keep your hearts and minds*
> *through Christ Jesus. (Philippians 4:6-7)*

Allow me to highlight two words in the aforementioned scripture; *careful* and *prayer*. In every situation we must choose prayer or care. By choosing prayer, we allow God to take care of our predicaments. Not choosing prayer burdens us with care.

The root derivative of the word care is the Greek word *merízō*. The word merízō means disunite, to take apart, or to separate. It is the same Greek word from which anxiety derives. Perpetually living in the state of care is mentally, physically and emotionally unhealthy. This is why the Bible admonishes us to cast all of our cares (anxieties, worries and fears) on the Lord (1 Peter 5:7). So, transform your mind from care to prayer.

Are you confronted with something presently pulling you apart? In ancient times torture was common practice. One

YOU DON'T HAVE TO LOSE YOUR MIND

torture tactic was particularly gruesome. The tormentors would tie a prisoner between two chariots. As the prisoner was fastened to chariots facing opposite directions, the horses were commanded to move. This would literally pull the prisoner in opposite directions simultaneously. Eventually, the tension would rip the person apart. Figuratively speaking, this is what care does. It pulls you in opposite directions until you are torn apart.

Do not allow fear, doubt and unbelief to tear you into pieces. Choose to transform your mind. Rather than trying to figure out a problem, give it to God and allow Him to work it out. It's your choice. Keep your mind and focus on the Lord. He is certainly able to correct the crooked things in your life.

Sometimes bad things happen to good people. There will be times when adversity meets you face-to-face. When this occurs, what do you do? How do you handle opposition? When you're given a pink slip at work; when the doctor offers a negative diagnosis; when your outflow exceeds your income, do you know where to turn? Better yet, to Whom do you turn?

People are being torn in all directions, because they choose care over prayer. Remember, the word care means to disunite, separate or take apart. So, when we are full of care it separates us from God. Subsequently, our lives will eventually disunite. Ultimately, the devil's plan is to dismantle our faith in the living God.

We ought to operate like David. His convictions led him to place faith in God even if the earth was removed from beneath his feet (Psalm 46:2). The Lord must remain first—before anything and everything. No matter what, we should choose prayer over care.

When we fold our hands, bow our heads and focus on God, we have contacted Him. Through prayer the Lord can rearrange the circumstances in our favor. Folding our hands represent the problem is no longer in our hands. We're admitting, "I can't handle this." We acknowledge any help we receive won't come from us, but from the Lord. Then we bow our heads in humility and close our eyes to stay focused on Him.

> *Thou wilt keep him in perfect peace, whose mind is stayed*
> *on thee: because he trusteth in thee. (Isaiah 26:3)*

Consider the words of our Lord as He sought to encourage His followers concerning the many trials they faced.

> *Therefore I say unto you,* **Take no thought for**
> **your life**, *what ye shall eat, or what ye shall*
> *drink; nor yet for your body, what ye shall put*
> *on. Is not the life more than meat, and the body*
> *than raiment? (Matthew 6:25 Bold Added)*

People today follow Jesus faithfully, but still lack faith. We can follow the Lord by attending church, studying the Bible and praying continuously. Sadly, we can do all these things and still not have faith in God.

When the Lord gave the instructions, "Take no thought" He was conveying, "Don't lose your mind."

Behold the fowls of the air: for they sow not,
neither do they reap, nor gather into barns;
yet your heavenly Father feedeth them. Are ye
not much better than they? (Matthew 6:26)

If you struggle having Christian faith, at least possess the bird's attitude toward life. Birds neither work nor save. Yet, our heavenly Father sees to it that they have provisions. Now, if the Lord provides for the birds (and He does) will He not take care of His children?

We do not have to be careful concerning our livelihood. God is going to prepare a table in the presence of our enemies. We may not know what the future holds, but we know Who holds the future. The Lord holds our future. So, don't lose your mind. Rather continue to transform your mind from care to prayer. Now, do you know what you should do after you pray?

METHOD OF REFORMING

And be not conformed to this world: but be ye transformed by the renewing of your mind, **that ye may prove what is that good, and acceptable, and perfect, will of God**. *(Romans 12:2 Bold Added)*

After you have transformed your mind through the practice of praying, you must reform your behavior by praising God. I hear people talking about finding the will of God for their lives. If you are still searching for God's will, allow me to suggest you start praising the Lord.

> *In every thing give thanks:* **for this is the will of God** *in Christ Jesus concerning you. (1 Thessalonians 5:18 Bold Added)*

No matter what happens to disrupt the flow of our everyday lives we must be mindful to give God thanks. Now, we're not thanking God for the issue, but we thank Him in the circumstance. This is evidence of our faith in Him. We give God thanks in the midst of any problem because we understand He will bring the solution.

The child of God does not have a perfect life; we just live a reformed life. We no longer desire to indulge in activities that bring shame to us or discredit the Lord. Our desire is now set on proving the good, acceptable and perfect will of God. We display a joyful disposition and a demonstration of praise.

> *Be careful for nothing; but in everything by prayer and supplication with thanksgiving let your requests be made known unto God." (Philippians 4:6)*

Prayer and supplication go together. Prayer is the vehicle to petition what we want from the Lord. Supplication is the means by which we receive God's will or what He expects from us. Do not miss this, following prayer and supplication, we are to make our requests known with thanksgiving.

Many people's requests are absent of thanksgiving. Thanksgiving is the course. It is the pathway leading to praise which is the force. Thanksgiving will always usher us into praise. I gratefully thank God every morning and when it's time to sleep at night.

The people who find it difficult to praise God are the same people who fail to give Him thanks. To segue from a problem to praise is a quantum leap. Thank the Lord when you're in a problem. This brings you to a confident state of mind. When we are able to appreciate the Lord, there is nothing that can oppose us and succeed. We position ourselves to give God praise. Thanking the Lord settles our spirit and we praise Him for solving the problem.

> *Rejoice in the Lord alway: and again*
> *I say, Rejoice. (Philippians 4:4)*

The method of reforming happens through thanksgiving, praise and joy. Thanksgiving is the course, praise is the force, and joy is the source. Thanksgiving helps us arrive at the point of giving God praise. However, we need joy on the inside to be thankful.

If you do not have joy, Paul commands you to, "rejoice." The prefix "re" carries the connotation "to do again." You can't repair something that was not fixed before. You cannot rejoice if you did not have joy from the beginning. Joy is a deep sense of inner strength and contentment, knowing God has adequate resources to fix any problem.

Some years ago, my wife Valerie went to our neighborhood park. She went there to meditate and spend time with the Lord. While sitting in her car the devil taunted Valerie with a thought. He told her she had a flat tire. Then he challenged her to give God praise in that negative circumstance.

Valerie exited the car to inspect the situation and sure enough, her tire was flat. After discovering the flat tire, she immediately began thanking the Lord and rejoicing. Valerie was thankful she had a cell phone whereby she could call for roadside assistance. Some people lose their mind when things go flat in their lives, but Valerie had a reason to rejoice.

My wife had a cell phone, roadside assistance, and a spare tire in the trunk of her car. And if all those resources were not enough, guess who pulled into the park next to her—yours truly, her faithful husband. Valerie did not have to lift a finger. All she had to do was praise the Lord. Beloved, Jesus will fix any flat you may incur in life.

In the midst of trauma, while you are weeping you can still

praise the Lord. Although your life may be falling to pieces and you're being pulled in many different directions, praise the Lord. Stand up! Clap your hands! Shout with the voice of triumph! Dance before the Lord! Whatever you do, don't quit on God and you will see, He will never quit on you.

> *And the peace of God, which surpasses all understanding, will guard your hearts and your minds in Christ Jesus. (Philippians 4:7)*

Remember our prayer must be coupled with praise. The consequence of prayer and praise is peace. Now, peace can't be bought in a bottle from the local drug store. You can buy a pill that will cause sleep, but peace is something only God can give.

> *Peace I leave with you, my peace I give unto you: not as the world giveth, give I unto you. Let not your heart be troubled, neither let it be afraid. (John 14:27)*

The world cannot give us peace and rest for our souls. However, the Lord desires to lift our burdens by removing our cares. Give God the things that pull you in different directions. You don't have to lose your mind. Pray, praise and do better.

CHAPTER ONE REFLECTIONS

Bad things happen to all people. No one is exempt from:

1. _____

2. _____

3. _____

Our outcome depends on our state _____ _____.

The human mind is the _____ where spiritual warfare takes place.

Losing one's _____ is the gateway to an unproductive life.

Moving from Conforming

Every day we have to choose to live above the common fray of this world's _____, _____, _____ ____, and the _____ that tries to pull us down.

We have to be careful not to allow _____ or _____ to create an arrogant mindset.

God wants us to develop the mind-set that if we lose everything we hold dear, but still have Him; we have _____ _____ _____ _____.

In a crisis we will either _____ the faith we have in God

or _____ more about the God we placed our faith in.

Motivated by Transforming

The process of transformation starts with us renewing our _____

_____.

The Lord wants us to renew our minds from a state of _____

_____ to a place of _____.

In every situation we must choose _____ or

_____.

Perpetually living in the state of care is _____,

_____ and _____ unhealthy.

Do not allow _____, _____ and

_____ to tear you into pieces.

Method of Reforming

No matter what happens to disrupt the flow of our everyday lives

we must be mindful to _____ _____.

The child of God does not have a perfect life; we just live a _____

_____ life.

Prayer and _____ go together.

The method of reforming happens through _____,

_____ and _____.

Thanksgiving is the _____, praise is the

_____, and joy is the _____.

You don't have to lose your mind. _____,

_____ and receive the Lord's _____.

FAITH FOR THE STORMS

*And the same day, when the even was come, he saith
unto them, Let us pass over unto the other side. And
when they had sent away the multitude, they took him
even as he was in the ship. And there were also with him
other little ships. And there arose a great storm of wind,
and the waves beat into the ship, so that it was now full.*
(Mark 4:35-37)

THE LORD WANTS our faith developed into a level of
confidence in Him. To accomplish His plan we must experience
adversity. We will never know God is capable of delivering us
from a storm until we find ourselves in the midst of one. Through
troublesome times, we seek God fervently and He responds
to our situations. Then, our faith is elevated to confidence
(1 Jhn 5:14-15).

According to the Bible we go from faith to faith (Rom.
1:17), strength to strength (Ps. 84:7) and glory to glory (2 Cor.
3:18). We progress through these spiritual phases by having
confidence in the living God.

When my daughter Nicole was fifteen, I taught her to drive. While in training, she had to become use to my every command. I gave her a series of instructions, "Both hands on the wheel, adjust the mirror, foot on the gas pedal, foot on the brake pedal." Like a hawk, my eyes were on her every move.

Once I felt her lessons were finished, I brought my wife Valerie to view her progress. I recall after I informed Valerie that Nicole could drive, my wife protested, "Oh my, now I have to worry about both of you on the road." I'll admit, Valerie still does not relax in the car when I'm driving.

Valerie got in the car and began shouting orders to Nicole, "Place both hands on the wheel. Look before you switch lanes. Place your signal on before turning. Come to a complete stop at the sign." After being drilled by her mother and me, Nicole became a pretty skilled motorist. There came a time when I would recline my seat, get relaxed and sleep while she was driving. I became confident in Nicole's driving skills.

Likewise, it takes faith to begin with God. However, after walking with Him for a while, we should progress from faith to confidence.

FROM FAITH TO CONFIDENCE

*For the which cause I also suffer these things: nevertheless I am not ashamed: for **I know** whom **I have believed**, and am persuaded that he is able to keep that which I have committed unto him against that day. (2 Timothy 1:12 Bold Added)*

The apostle Paul expressed in the previous scripture, "I know" which connotes confidence. He said he knew the God he once "believed." Like Paul, you need to move from believing to living by faith. Faith is acting on what you believe. Afterwards, you will come into an experience with God. Through actual experience you will gain a new found confidence in God's ability to deliver you from what appears to be impossible.

Jesus said in the world we will have tribulations (three times the trouble). The Lord illustrated the rains descended, the floods came, and the winds beated against the houses of the obedient, as well as, the disobedient. The person whose house fell refused God's Word, while the house of the person that received God's Word stood (Matt. 7:24-27).

The storm did not cause the house to collapse. However, a lack of faith did. Both houses had to withstand the tempest. The house left standing was built on the right stuff—God's Word. No one is exempt from trials of life. We must have faith in God. For this reason, God provided His church and preacher. The preacher's job is to establish the people's belief system. The pastor must not pretend, fabricate or project fantasies in the minds of people. As a pastor my job is to convince people to believe.

While attending my oldest grand-daughter's graduation from a performing arts college in New York City, an acting director gave the commencement address. He exclaimed, "If you are a true actor, make believe!" I looked at Valerie and said,

"That's my job; that's what I've been assigned by God to do—make His people believe in Him."

There was a little boy who sat in Sunday school. The teacher asked for someone to give the definition of faith. The little boy raised his hand and said, "Faith is making believe what you know is not so." Now, that's not faith. Faith is not making believe what you know is not so. Faith is acting on what God says is so.

Listen to this account of two brothers. One was a preacher, the other a lawyer. The preacher could not seem to get anyone to join the church. Even worse, his parishioners would not faithfully attend the church. Coincidently, his church failed to grow.

On the other hand, the lawyer had clients everywhere waiting for his services. So, the preacher contacted his successful brother and said, "I'm doing something wrong. I need you to come to my church and assess my situation. The attorney said, "I will be glad to help you."

The lawyer went to his brother's church service to hear him preach. Afterwards, the preacher enquired of him, "Did you notice anything?" The attorney said, "Oh it's as plain as the nose on your face." Surprised, the preacher beckoned, "What is it?" The attorney remarked with confidence, "See, I tell lies like they are true. You tell truths like they are lies."

Moving from faith to confidence means we must live according to the truth of God's Word. The devil is the father of lies, even when he pulls the wool over your eyes ninety-nine percent is nylon. So, don't believe his false report. When the storms come to your house stand and speak God's Word.

There was an extremely wealthy man who attended church. The affluent fella didn't necessarily believe that God was a living, active authority. Yet, he believed a higher source created our universe. One day after church concluded someone asked the tycoon, "Why do you attend church when you don't believe in God?" The wealthy man's response was, "Although I don't truly believe in God, the preacher talks as though he does."

We should live in such a way that others will follow Jesus. Displaying belief in the Lord is best when the storms of life challenge us to our very core. When we reach our core there should only be confidence.

We begin with having faith in God. Through adversity we gain experience. By experience we obtain confidence. Our confidence is in knowing the Lord will get us through every storm.

FAITH TO GET THROUGH THE STORM

God can get us through any storm. We will never know God's power until we are faced with an insurmountable problem. God can instruct us out of every predicament. However, we will not receive God's instructions without first receiving His correction. Through correction we are able to straighten the crooked things in our lives. More importantly, we must have an ear to hear what the Lord is speaking.

Jesus taught His disciples that a sower went forth to sow (Matt. 13:3). In His parable, the seed sown was God's Word. There were four types of ground at the farmer's disposal. Each ground represented the various people who were given God's Word. Let's consider each ground/hearer.

The Way Side is symbolic of the person who totally pays no attention to God's Word. You can preach until your face turns blue and this person never receives the message. The Word of God never gets in this individual.

The Stony Place is symbolic of the shallow person. This individual lacks depth in their spirituality. Therefore, the challenges of life strip them of the Word they receive. The Word gets inside this kind of person, but it fails to go down because of their superficiality.

The Thorns symbolize the person that's carnal. This person is worrisome and has no real faith in God. They allow the cares of this world to cancel the Word of God they hear. The Word gets in this person and down into their soul, but their fears never allow them to bring the Word forth. In essence, they hear the Word, but never speak God's Word.

The Good Ground represents the person who hears and believes God's Word. This individual experiences trials, yet gains confidence. They speak God's Word and produce fruit on various levels in their life. With this person, God's Word gets in, goes down, comes up and produces positive results.

Now hear this, every storm in our life is not caused by Satan. Sometimes God causes storms. However, His purpose is not to destroy you, but to bring about your spiritual enhancement. The source or force of the storm really does not matter. The deciding factor is the course we take through the storm. We must choose to follow God because He is able to make all things work together for our good.

You have to decide you will not be the way side, stony place or thorny ground. Become the good ground the Lord can plant his Word inside to bring about beneficial change for others. God desires to get you through your storms so you may help other people through theirs.

Getting through our storms will take praying to God. Many people fail to pray because they do not see immediate results. Nevertheless, there needs to be an understanding that like a master chef, God is in the kitchen cooking and preparing what we need. The Lord is not a short-order cook just whipping up quick answers. Even more, He is not preparing the promised life for us, but rather us for the promised life.

Along with the promised life we receive kingdom keys. Jesus authorized us to handle these keys. They should be utilized in our prayer life. We discover through the Word of God what we bind on earth will be bound in heaven. Likewise, the things we loose in prayer will be loosed in heaven. The power of binding and loosening can only take place in our prayer life. Also, there must be an understanding that we are given keys and we do not create keys of our own.

To handle the kingdom keys involves the ability to hear from God. Thus, when we bind something in the natural realm, it must already be bound in the spiritual realm. In essence, we take our cues from the Word of God. The Bible says Elijah caused it not to rain. His ability to bind the rain was a result of God's law. This law issued a stiff punishment for the disobedience of Israel—no rain for three years.

By possessing the kingdom keys we can pray, "Thy kingdom come, Thy will be done on earth as in heaven." Through spending time in God's Word and a devoted prayer life, the Lord will get us through the storms. Placing our faith in the living God is always the best option. It strengthens us before, through and after the storms. Thereby, we become testimonies of God's goodness.

FAITH TO BELIEVE AND RECEIVE FROM GOD

And the same day, when the even was come, he saith unto them, Let us pass over unto the other side. And when they had sent away the multitude **they took him even as he was** *in the ship. And there were also with him other little ships. And there arose a great storm of wind, and the waves beat into the ship, so that it was now full. And*

he was in the hinder part of the ship, asleep on a pillow:
and they awake him, and say unto him, Master, carest
thou not that we perish? (Mark 4:35-38 Bold Added)

We must have faith in God before the storms of life approach. Interestingly, this account said the disciples *took Jesus as He was* into their boat. Do we do that today? Do we take God according to His divine nature or do we attribute human characteristics to Him?

Let's examine the way you take the Lord. When you're facing deadlines do you tell God, "There's no more time." When the doctor gives you a negative report do you say, "Lord, there's nothing that can be done?" How about when the bills are high and the funds low, do you confess, "I'll never be able to afford any of life's pleasures." You do not speak this way when you take Jesus as He is. In spite of life's setbacks God is watching and waiting for the right time to release His blessings.

God gave us faith so we may use it to receive whatever we need. To know God is to understand He has the power to deliver us from any problem. However, rather than delivering us from the problem, He chooses to use the problem to develop us.

There is a key to receive what you need from God and that key is your faith in Him. You must believe in God's ability to succeed rather than your own inability to fail. Take your eyes off of yourself and place them on the Lord.

*Who being the brightness of his glory, and the express
image of his person, and* **upholding all things by
the word of his power**. *(Hebrews 1:3 Bold Added)*

Placing your eyes on the Lord enables you to see problems
as potential for God's power. The power of God is in His Word.
When God speaks, His power is generated.

There were ten lepers who cried to Jesus for healing (Lu.
17:12-14). Jesus heard their plea for release from pain and granted
their request along with instructions. Jesus told the lepers to
show themselves to the priest. Now, in order for them to show
themselves to the priest they needed to be healed. Understand,
their healing came as a result of their obedience. The Bible emphatically declares they were cleansed as they followed the Lord's
instructions.

It took faith for them to believe they were healed based on
God's word. No one said, "I don't feel healed." Being lepers came
with discouragement and disappointments. Putting emotions aside,
they all looked for the priests. As they walked in God's direction
they received the Lord's correction. Their leprosy was replaced
with healing, their believing brought about their receiving.

Faith does not just believe who He is; faith is receiving the
Word He says. Having faith means receiving how God sends His
Word. Some people come to church and they believe who He is,
but they don't receive the way He chooses to send His message.

You can't get a Word unless God gives you a voice. The

preacher is God's voice. The Apostle John declared, "I am the voice" (Jhn. 1:23). God can't speak a Word unless there is a voice. As the preacher is speaking, the Holy Spirit is making the Word of God relevant to the hearers. The Spirit of the Lord reveals everything will be alright because He holds all things together by His powerful Word (Heb. 1:3).

God wants us to see His greatness, goodness and grace. He must be recognized as God alone. Listen, if you know Him as God before the storm, allow Him to remain God during the storm. Never allow the circumstance to dictate how far you'll walk with God in faith.

Like the ten lepers, the Lord wants us to walk by faith and not by sight or feelings. Many people fail to follow God's orders today because they do not see their desired results. Sometimes it becomes difficult to see the way out of a problem. Nevertheless, when we take our eyes off the problem and place them on the Solution (Jesus), we receive the light.

When the Lord gives instructions, don't doubt Him. If God says a fly can pull a buggy, just hook him up! Get ready, you're about to witness a miracle. Don't doubt you can be what God says you can be. Don't doubt you can have what God says you can have. Don't doubt you can live where God says you can live. If you believe, by faith you will receive.

Whenever you are caught in the storms of life, there's no need to fear; confess by faith, "I'm doing better!" The Lord is in control, and the storms will subside.

CHAPTER TWO REFLECTIONS

The Lord wants our faith developed into a level of _____

_____ in Him.

According to the Bible we go from _____ to

_____ (Rom. 1:17), _____ to

_____ (Ps. 84:7) and _____

to _____ (2 Cor. 3:18).

From Faith to Confidence

Faith is acting on what you _____.

God provided His _____ and _____

_____.

The preacher's job is to establish the people's _____

_____ system.

Moving from faith to confidence means we must live according

to the truth of God's _____.

Through adversity we gain _____.

By experience we obtain _____.

Faith to Get Through the Storm

We will never know God's _____ until we are

faced with an insurmountable _____.

We will not receive God's _____ without

first receiving His _____.

There were four types of ground at the farmer's disposal. Each

ground represented the various people who were given God's

Word (Matt. 13:3).

The _____ symbolize the person that's carnal.

This person is worrisome and has no real faith in God.

The _____ _____ is symbolic of the person

who totally pays no attention to God's Word.

The _____ _____ represents the per-

son who hears and believes God's Word.

The _____ _____ is symbolic of the

shallow person. This individual lacks depth in their spirituality.

Now hear this, every storm in our life is not caused by _____

_____. Sometimes _____ causes storms.

Getting through our storms will take _____

_____ to God.

To handle the kingdom keys involves the ability to _____

from God.

Faith to Believe and Receive from God

God gave us _____ so we may use it to receive

whatever we need.

You must believe in God's ability to _____

rather than your own inability to _____.

Placing your eyes on the Lord enables you to see _____

_____ as potential for God's _____

_____.

You can't get a Word unless God gives you a _____.

The _____ is God's voice.

Listen, if you know Him as God _____ the storm,

allow Him to remain God _____ the storm.

CHAPTER THREE

WHEN YOU'RE DOWN TO NOTHING GOD IS UP TO SOMETHING

And a certain woman, which had an issue of blood twelve years, And had suffered many things of many physicians, and had spent all that she had, and was nothing bettered, but rather grew worse.
(Mark 5:25-26)

THE WOMAN in the opening passage had issues. Her issues were not the worse of her condition. It became really bad for her because she spent all her wealth trying to improve her health and to no avail. Her case is not unlike many of the situations that surround us today.

You might be familiar with her predicament. Have you watch your finances diminish, business fail or family fall apart? What do you do when you have exhausted all options? Where do you turn when the people you relied on let you down? How do you get back up when the heavy weight of disappointment comes crashing down? You want to know what to do? Where to go? Who to turn to? Well, why not follow the example set by this woman with the issue. She went to Jesus.

Beloved, it's important to know, when you're down to nothing, God is up to something.

There was another woman with a similar account. She was in church. More than likely she was in dire straits and no doubt came to receive a word of encouragement. I'm sure the service went smooth without a hitch. I can imagine the announcements were inviting, the choir exciting and the sermon igniting. Then came the time many people look toward the exits—financial giving.

Everyone made their way to the offering plate. Many people gave from their surplus. Even more parishioners dropped money into the church container without giving it a second thought. They gave carelessly just because what they gave placed no financial dent in their pocket. However, the woman did not give much by many standards, but by God's estimation her giving was enough to stop the service.

This woman was down to her last two coins. Someone may wonder, how much would her coins be worth in today's market? Honestly, it does not matter. Jesus did not seek to draw attention to the woman's finances, but to her faith. He said she gave more than anyone else in the service. It's not that she gave the most monetarily; she gave the most because she did not consider her condition as a cause not to give. She saw it as a reason to give. This woman trusted that as she provided for God's house He would reciprocate and provide for her house.

When you evaluate your issues, are you counting your coins or counting on the Lord? The next time you are experiencing a setback know it's God pulling you back to sling-shot you forward to your blessing. So, don't complain when things look bad; rather take the opportunity to raise a higher praise to the Lord.

RAISE A HIGHER PRAISE

Too often I hear people complain about their condition. These disgruntled disciples of the Lord talk as if God is not concerned with the plight of His people. Somehow, they believe God does not understand their pain. However, this is not true. God totally comprehends our pain, but it does not stop with His comprehension, He is moved with compassion.

Due to the failure of Adam, sin had a death-grip on humanity. God knew all of humanity would die and be eternally separated from Him. However, God counteracted the cause of sin with the cure—Jesus. In essence, God bankrupted heaven to buy back our life and liberty. When God offered Jesus He was not down to His last option, He gave His only option.

The day Jesus died on earth, God spent all He had and would do it all again because of His love for us. Jesus died and was buried, but that's not the end of the account. When the devil took his best shot; God came with one even better—Jesus' resurrection.

Jesus was in the ground for three days and three nights, but on the third day He rose from the dead. This is why we praise the Lord. When situations pile on us and debt, disease, and discomfort bury us, the only way up and out is to raise the praise. You may argue, "I tried praising God and nothing happened." To that argument I appeal, "Raise the praise higher!"

Never give the devil the last word. When he speaks, you speak louder. When the enemy taunts how you're down to nothing, draw back your shoulders and remind him that your God is up to something. Always remember, it's not over until God say's it's over. When the clock strikes midnight—it's not over. When the job gives you the pink slip—it's not over. Don't even listen when the fat lady sings because—it's—not—over! When the devil brings his banner of defeat, you raise a higher praise.

It's favor time for the people of God. During your difficulty the Lord will bring honey out of a rock. A rock is one of the hardest natural substances. Honey happens to be one of the sweetest natural substances. Jesus is our Rock and God brings honey out of Him. When times are tough, go to Jesus.

Whatever you are doing for God, don't stop. Multiply His praise and amplify His glory. Despite the hardships, don't tone it down, this is your moment to lift your praise. Don't let the devil shut you up; raise a higher praise!

It is important for us to reflect on our past in order to appreciate how far we have come. God has brought us through heartaches, disappointments, and mistreatment. He has given us victory by allowing us to accomplish many of our goals. Even still, His plan for us is not complete. There are more mountains to scale and roads to explore. Although our journey is not without pain, we overcome every obstacle through praise.

Don't become preoccupied by the negatives, keep your eyes on the positives. Focus your attention on Jesus who is the Author and the Finisher of our faith (Heb. 12:2). Right now the economy is unstable and our communities are shaken by crime. Yet, you do not have to stumble or fall because when it appears nothing is happening in the natural realm, something is taking place in the spiritual arena.

SOMETHING IS GETTING READY TO HAPPEN

Hard times occur to teach and train us. It's been said, "That which does not kill you makes you stronger." During the tough times, we discover what we are made of. When darkness overtakes us we don't have to panic. We need to do in the dark what we did in the light—speak God's Word. When you are down to nothing God is up to something. Wait in faith knowing something is getting ready to happen.

> *And a certain woman, which had an issue of blood twelve years, And had suffered many things of many physicians, and had spent all that she had, and was nothing bettered, but rather grew worse,* **When she had heard of Jesus, came in the press behind***, and touched his garment. (Mark 5:25-27 Bold Added)*

This woman heard of Jesus and coupled her hearing with her action. She came in the press. The press was the throngs of people who followed Jesus. Coming in the midst of the people was risky and could be fatal. The Law of Moses declared her unclean. Therefore, she was not permitted to be in social settings and being caught was a death sentence. However, desperate people do desperate things.

Sometimes it takes us being desperate enough to get what we need from God. The casual can come late for the cure. The nonchalant can miss the move of God. But when we know something is getting ready to happen, we tend to prepare for it.

Many of God's people have become discouraged because their prayer request failed to manifest. In many instances, it's not that God has not heard your prayer nor is He ignoring your prayer. I believe He's waiting for many people to get into position.

Consider the game of baseball. This sport is governed by a set of rules. The guidelines for baseball state you need a player on home plate with a bat. You also need a pitcher on the mound with a ball. Finally, you need a catcher positioned behind the batter with a glove ready to catch the ball that the pitcher throws. In order to commence the game the aforementioned players and equipment are essential.

Now, the pitcher can't just throw the ball anytime he's ready. He must wait until the batter steps into the batter's box. Even then, he will not throw the ball. The pitcher waits for the catcher to send a signal indicating the desired pitch. The pitcher can agree or disagree with the catcher's request. Finally, when the pitcher recognizes that the catcher is in position, he throws the ball to his catcher. The job of the batter is to disrupt the pitcher and catcher by hitting the ball.

Using this analogy, God is the pitcher, the devil is the batter and you are the catcher. First, you send a signal to God in prayer. God receives your signal and decides to pitch your prayer request. However, the devil stands between you and the Lord with his bat trying to knock your prayer request out of sight. To those not familiar with the sport, it appears the pitcher is throwing the ball to the batter, but he isn't; the ball is thrown to the catcher. Now, God is not considering the devil at bat, He's waiting for you as the catcher to get into position.

Are you in position with your glove ready to receive your blessings? You are when you understand something is getting ready to happen. Someone said when you pray you must P.U.S.H (pray until something happens). I sense in the spiritual realm God is aligning things for His people.

Listen, if it can happen anywhere it can happen here. If it can happen at any time it can happen now. If it can happen to anyone it can happen to you. Now, if you believe that get into position.

When the woman heard of Jesus she came in His presence. Her faith kicked into another gear and she was ready to take her blessing. I'm not conveying we take anything from God. Whatever we acquire from the Lord must be received. Nevertheless, we can take what belongs to us from the enemy. The devil is trying to hold back your healing, children and prosperity. Albeit, you can take back your stuff with authority because the Lord has authority over Satan and his demons.

The Bible records an account when Jesus had to deal with demons that terrorized a man. Jesus told His disciples to enter their boat for a little trip. The weather was pleasant as the Lord dispersed His plan. However, conditions took a turn for the worse as they ventured toward their destination. The boat was tested for its strength, the disciples for their faith. Through it all, Jesus gave a command of peace and the weather became calm.

Once they reached their destination, Jesus and His crew were confronted by a demonically possessed man. This man was cast out of society and chained in a place of solitude. No one had been in communication with him for quite some time.

When it came to those who knew him, this man was out of touch, out of sight and out of his mind. However, he was never out of the reach of God.

The Lord knew this man was crying on the inside and desperate for help to find him on the outside. The disciples were totally unaware of this demonized man. They had no clue that defeating demons was on Jesus' agenda. However, the Lord knew the man's place and pain.

Although, Jesus gave His disciples the ability to cast out devils, this man was occupied by a legion. He was aggravated and aggressive, so people left him alone. However, the demons could not hold this guy back when he saw Jesus. Even with internal bondage, he ran and fell at Jesus' feet. Jesus casted the devils out of that man and into a herd of swine; the next time this man was in the company of others he was clothed, and in his right mind.

When you are down to nothing God is up to something. God can deliver you through any dilemma. He is greater than any problem you will face in this world (1 John 4:4). Every time the devil is defeated God gets the glory and you have a story.

HIS GLORY: YOUR STORY

We all have a responsibility to tell what the Lord has done for us. It is spiritually criminal for a Christian to say they know Christ, but they have no joy. When things are looking down, you must know how to lift up your head. You do this by looking toward the Lord because He's the glory and lifter of your head (Psalm 3:3). The joy of the Lord gives you strength (Neh. 8:10). So, you don't have a right to sit on the testimony of the Lord. You don't have a right to shut your mouth and not lift your voice to give Him praise. If God has done something for you, tell somebody.

God never promised we would not experience hardship. He has not promised us prevention, but protection. We have to serve the devil notice that the Lord is our Shepherd and we will not want. Even when we walk through the proverbial valley of the shadow of death, we will fear no evil because our God is with us (Psalm 23:4). We ought to tell somebody our story so God can get His glory.

David wrote how his heart was fixed trusting in the Lord (Ps. 112:8). However, David did not always sit on a throne. Sometimes we can think when someone is strong in the Lord they have always been that way. Yet, this is not true and it certainly was not the case with David.

When David penned the 23rd Psalm he was going through a valley in his life (Ps. 23:4). A valley is a test. It's a place that you would like to change if you could change it. However, since you can't change a valley you have to go through it. Even still, you can let the devil know the Lord is the Lily in the valleys. In other words, when you're down to nothing, God is up to something. He will bring you down in the valley, only to teach you something about Him. Once the valley test is concluded, get ready because He will take you up for a mountain top experience.

God can take you from the valleys to the mountains and He can change your water into wine. Mary was catering a wedding when suddenly a problem occurred. The wine supply had vanished. The reception comprised a list of "Who's who." Hence, running out of wine meant someone's job was on the line. Therefore, Mary told Jesus the problem and told the servants to stand by for the solution.

Does God really care about our wine racks, broken air conditioners, missing golf clubs or any of the other things that could be listed as trivial pursuits? I don't know if God cares about many of the things that keep us up at night, but I'm certain of this—He loves us. Therefore, He takes care of the things that concern us (Ps. 138:8). The Lord is full of compassion and His mercy is boundless.

God has pity for His children (Ps. 103:13). He sees our tears, hears our cries and understands our sorrows. When we are down to nothing, He meets us where we are to elevate us where He is. The purpose for the problems is to give us a story, but His help gives Him the glory. So don't rob Him of the glory by failing to seek Him for the answer.

When facing their dilemma, Mary instructed the servants to do whatever Jesus commanded. Faith follows the Lord's instructions to the letter. The problem for many of God's people is disobedience. God gives the answer and they struggle with the follow-through. The answer may not be what they expected, but it's the answer nonetheless.

Jesus told the servants to fill large water pots with water and take it to the governor. Now, talk about adding insult to injury. Running out of wine was one thing; substituting water for wine was ludicrous. And still, Jesus gave the command and the servants had to obey if they wanted to see a miracle take place.

The Lord could have stood up and made a scene by openly transforming water to wine. However, God knew they needed a miracle not a spectacle. Too often, we miss God's miracles because we seek the spectacular. The Lord cares more about discipline than He does displaying His power. Our faith in God is shown by saying, giving or doing something. Jesus wanted the servants to exercise their faith by doing something.

Then came the moment of truth; the governor sipped from the new batch that was given to Him. Like a connoisseur, the governor made a proclamation after swallowing the drink. He said, "Everyone usually serves the worst wine last, but you have saved the best wine for last!" the amount of wine they began with was not enough to sustain the celebration. However, when they gave their issue to the Lord, He provided more than enough to meet their need. When you feel dry and unfulfilled, turn to Jesus; He has wine (joy) that sustains and satisfies.

Beloved, do not despise hardships. The Lord allows hardness in our lives to teach us. If you allow Him, God will bring sweetness out of hardness and honey out of the rock. Hard times will either break or make you. Those who accept Jesus Christ are saved by grace, but sons are made by growth.

Do you want to be a son of God? Do you want to walk and talk with Him? It's one thing for God to walk with you. He will never leave you, but God allows some people to walk with Him. Walking with the Lord takes maturity and maturity manifests through hardships. The Lord desires to take you where you've never been, show you things you've never seen and give you experiences you've never had.

What's your story? You have a story and a responsibility to report it. I read the following some years ago and find it applicable for the moment:

> *You write the fifth gospel, a chapter every day,*
> *by the deeds that you do and the words that you*
> *say. Men read what you do whether faithless or*
> *true, what is the gospel according to you?*

When troubles seem to surround you raise your praise. When life appears mundane, look for the shift because something is getting ready to happen. Your story is for God's glory. So, He is looking for you to tell others of His goodness in your life. Above all, remember when you are down to nothing, God is up to something. He's making a way for you to do better.

CHAPTER THREE REFLECTION

Beloved, it's important to know, when you're _____ _____

_____, God is _____ _____ _____.

Don't complain when things look bad; rather take the opportuni-

ty to _____ a higher _____ to the Lord.

Raise a Higher Praise

God totally comprehends our pain, but it does not stop with His

_____, He is moved with _____.

God counteracted the cause of sin with the cure— _____.

When God offered Jesus He was not down to His _____

option, He gave His _____ option.

When situations pile on us and debt, disease, and discomfort

bury us, the only way up and out is to _____ the

_____.

During your difficulty the Lord will bring _____

out of a rock.

Whatever you are doing for God, don't stop. _____

His praise and _____ His glory.

Don't become preoccupied by the _____, keep

your eyes on the _____.

Something is Getting Ready to Happen

We need to do in the dark what we did in the light— _____

_____ _____ _____

_____.

When you are down to _____ God is up

to _____.

Using this analogy of baseball, God is the _____, the

devil is the _____ and you are the _____.

Someone said when you pray you must P.U.S.H. The acronym for

is _____ _____ _____

_____.

Listen, if it can happen anywhere it can happen _____.

If it can happen at any time it can happen _____.

If it can happen to anyone it can happen to _____.

Every time the devil is defeated God gets the _____ and

you have a _____.

His Glory: Your Story

It is spiritually criminal for a Christian to say they know Christ, but

they have no _____.

God never promised we would not experience hardship. He has

not promised us _____, but _____.

God can take you from the valleys to the _____

and He can change your water into _____.

The purpose for the problems is to give us a _____,

but His help gives Him the _____.

Our faith in God is shown by _____,

_____ or _____ something.

If you allow Him, God will bring _____ out of

hardness and _____ out of the rock.

Those who accept Jesus Christ are saved by _____,

but sons are made by _____.

Walking with the Lord takes _____ and maturity

manifests through _____.

Your story is for God's _____.

STAYING IN THE POSITIVE LANE

A MAGNIFIER IS A GLASS that enlarges objects. I'll admit the older I get the more I appreciate its use. The human mind can serve as magnifiers. When we meditate on any particular person, place or thing, they become enlarged. As a nation, Israel magnified their problems not their God (Ps. 78:19). As a result, they placed restrictions on the Lord. The Bible conveys, "They limited the Holy One of Israel" (Ps. 78:41).

The Lord is the source of our satisfaction and the solution for every problem we face. He wants us to seek Him early in the morning, consider Him throughout the course of our day and close our eyes at night secure in His love. The only way to accomplish this is by staying in the positive lane.

Whenever I travel on a highway with multiple lanes I'm intrigued at the many cars that are traveling in the same direction. Not everyone has the same destination. Some people are on the highway for extensive miles while other people are merely traveling shorter distances. Whether traveling far or not, the important element is to stay in your lane.

People cross lanes all the time on the highway and sometimes to the displeasure of other commuters. Whenever I'm traveling to unfamiliar places I am cognizant of staying in the proper lane. For instance, I am notified of which lane to drive in by my GPS system. I could be traveling in the far left lane and the navigation system will warn me to get in the right lane in order to continue on the desired path.

In life it's so easy to get into the wrong lane. You can travel in the improper lane if you do not know where you're going. Even worse, you can get in a lane that exits the highway before you would like. We avoid unexpected exits in life by keeping our focus on our purpose and staying in the positive lane. More importantly, staying in the positive lane consists of having positive, possibility and principle thinking.

POSITIVE THINKING

There were two buckets in a well. One bucket was always happy and singing with gladness. The other bucket was always sad, mad, doomy and gloomy. This bucket remarked to the happy bucket, "I don't understand you." The joyful bucket responded, "What is it that you don't understand about me?" The sad bucket replied, "How come you're always glad? How come you're always singing? How come you are always happy?"

Surprised by his questions, the happy bucket then responded, "I don't understand you. How come you are always sad, mad, doomy and gloomy?" Now really upset, the negative bucket retorted, "I'll tell you the reason I'm always sad, mad, gloomy and doomy. Don't you see where we are? Don't you see we are in this deep dark tunnel of a well? And, no matter how full I go up I always come down empty." With the final word, the positive bucket countered, "Oh, I'll tell you the reason why I am always happy and singing with glee. I see that we are in this dark, deep tunnel of a well, but no matter how empty I come down I always go up full!"

We must get beyond negativity if we are going to be what God would have us to be. Negativity like gravity will pull you down. To be a positive person, you must go against the trend of the world. Positive people can't just float downstream. They must reverse the curse of the world's system and exert spiritual effort opposite the world's direction.

The way of the world is opposite the way of God. The world promotes being first, but Jesus taught being last. The world creates an insatiable appetite to get, but the Lord encourages us to give. For the person who wants to live, God reveals we must first die. The world's philosophy dictates, "Get all you can, then can all you get; sit on the top and let the rest rot." This philosophy carries a negative and selfish mentality. However, with God we must remain positive.

Staying in the positive lane keeps us on the right course. Being in the negative lane causes us to travel in the wrong direction. Negativity pulls us out of God's presence and prohibits us from receiving His promise. That is where the nation of Israel found itself after finally reaching the Promised Land.

God delivered Israel from captivity in Egypt. Yet, deliverance was just a part of God's plan. The Lord desired to bring His people to a place of prosperity. Now, to do this would prove difficult for Israel. Prosperity is the place for those who think positively. Some people can never become prosperous because they cannot perceive their situation getting better.

Israel lived in the wilderness as nomads for forty years. During those years, God proved He could provide for His people. Then it finally happened, Israel reached the borders of the Promised Land. Rather than walking straight in and trusting God to protect and provide as He had always done, Moses decided to send ahead a scouting party. The team's assignment was to survey the territory and report their findings back to Moses and the people.

Moses sent twelve spies to assess the area and after days of calculating the land the spies returned with their report. Ten spies returned with a negative report, but two spies (Joshua and Caleb) surrendered a positive report.

How is this possible? If all twelve traveled to the same locations, what caused the conflicting accounts? The answer is discovered in the difference between negative and positive thinkers.

All twelve of the spies saw the same thing; but they all did not see the same thing the same way. The ten saw the same thing the two saw, but the two didn't see it the same way the ten saw it. They were in the same environment at the same time. However, ten spies came back and said, "We are not able," and two spies said, "We are able." The ten spies considered their own strength and settled on negativity. The two spies recognized the power of God. They understood God's ability not their own.

Positive thinking is not wishful thinking. Joshua and Caleb were not simply wishing God would help them; their thinking was based on past experiences. The Lord took Israel on a path that was occupied by enemy forces. On the way to the Promised Land God toppled one opposing nation after another. Therefore, the two spies had no reason to believe Canaan (the Promised Land) would be any different.

When God gives you a promise you best believe He's not counting on you to perform it. The Lord's promises are predicated on His ability not your ability. When problems cause us to have a negative attitude we are conveying our unbelief in God. Positive thinking stems from an awareness that no matter the situation God can deliver and direct us.

Israel's problem stemmed from their self-perspective. They saw themselves through a negative lens. Negativity is contagious. Practically the entire nation adopted the ten spies' negative viewpoint and Moses received the two spies' positive perspective. The ten spies said, "We are not able" the two spies belted, "We are able!" Who was right? Both groups were right. The people who said, "We are not" were not; the men who said, "We are well able" were able and did receive God's promise.

The Promised Land was preoccupied with giants. Well, I hear someone asking, "Why didn't God warn them about the giants?" The answer is simple, when God doesn't mention it, it doesn't matter. To Israel the inhabitants of the land were too big to face. You may be like Israel facing overwhelming obstacles. If you understand, God is bigger when you look through the eyes of faith. Without the Lord many things can appear impossible, but with Him on your side all things become possible.

POSSIBILITY THINKING

Possibility thinking prepares us to do better in life. Many times doing better entails taking risks. God will call us to places we never thought of going, meeting people we never imagined coming in contact with and it will take utilizing our faith. Faith obeys God's Word even when we cannot understand or determine the outcome.

There were two children named Donny and Johnny. Their mom told them to go outside and see how much gas was in the car so they could go to grandmother's house. They finished breakfast and ran out of the house as fast as they could. Donny came back in the house, dragging, sagging and lagging, "Mom, we're not going to Grandma's house today, because the car is half empty." Johnny said, "Mommy, we can go to grandma's house today. The car is half-full!"

Johnny saw the car as half-full and that was enough to make the trip. Possibility thinking sees things from a unique perspective. When other people are complaining about disadvantages the people who see possibilities take advantage of any given situation. It's how you see it. Some see life as half empty; others see it as half-full. Some say concerning their journey, "We are almost there" while other say, "We'll never get there." How a person sees is based on their belief and sooner or later their belief system is revealed through their speech.

The words you speak come from what you believe. Your belief comes from what you think. How you think is based on your source. There are only two sources from which we draw information, the devil and God. The devil will look to convince you that there's no use trying in life. He will bring all your inadequacies to mind. On the other hand, the Lord will remind you the answer is found in Him not yourself. After considering Jesus and His awesomeness you have to conclude all things are possible.

63

God cannot take some people with Him because they won't have a heart to believe in Him. True faith is not God getting you out of something; it's God walking you into something. The Lord is bringing you to a problem. God will walk you through an obstacle so that He can show Himself strong.

People who think "All things are possible" have learned to wait on the Lord. They do not allow their strength to be sapped. These people can believe the Lord for their healing, deliverance and break-through. They confess to be the head and not the tail, above only and not beneath. Their lifestyle is reflective of their faith in God.

So many people make excuses why they have not succeeded. They will tell you all the things their parents failed to do. As a result, their circumstances have become negative. When we have our hope in the Lord, we pack all excuses away in a chest. Then we bury the chest with no intensions of it ever resurfacing.

I can't! It will never happen for me! That's impossible! All these negative terms have no room in the life of a person with possibility thinking. In fact, without God the word is impossible, but with God it becomes *I'm possible*. If God be for you, who can be against you? God is for you so that's good. However, if God is against you, that's bad.

When you are for someone you are considered a fan. When your support for the person causes others to support them you can be called a cheerleader. Cheerleaders are important in the world of sports. Although they do not actually play the game, their encouragement can provide strength to the players.

Did you know you have a fan? Not just a fan, but a cheerleader. You may have never considered it, but God is your biggest fan. His cheerleading causes angels to support you as well. God is for you. He has angels encamped around you for your protection. More importantly, He sent Jesus to defeat the devil. Now, any opposition you confront has been rendered ineffective. In other words, God has rigged the game so you will win.

What difficulty are you facing right now? If you have a loved one undergoing treatment in a medical center say, "God is for me." If you have to go through surgery and the doctor lists the risk chart, "God is with me." When your child is struggling with their identity and begins to show disrespect, just say, "God is in me." In every situation remind yourself that all things are possible to overcome when God is by your side.

Staying in the positive lane is not always easy, but can be accomplished through possibility thinking. When facing troubled times you will see hope because you know you have help. The same situations that will cause others to stumble will become a source of strength for you. You will come to understand the Lord uses hardships to develop your faith. Through faith all things are possible and we learn to lean on the Lord's principles.

PRINCIPLE THINKING

And there we saw the giants, the sons of Anak,
which come of the giants: and we **were in our**
own sight as grasshoppers, *and so we were*
in their sight. (Numbers 13:33 Bold Added)

God brought Israel out of Egypt, but believe it or not, that was the easy part. It was even more difficult to get Egypt out of them. They carried the negative lessons and bad habits through the wilderness like luggage. The Lord gave them a promise of living the good life, but to obtain God's kind of life would mean living by the Lord's principle.

The Lord has one key principle in which all other principles rest and that is believe in Him. Israel complained throughout their wilderness journey. When they complained of thirst, God provided water from a rock. Every time their stomachs grumbled, God gave them food from heaven. Every nation that stood in the way of their progress, the Lord provided power to have them removed. Now the moment of truth, Israel was on the cusp of entering their Promised Land, but one thing stood in their way—pessimism.

Israel received the report from the ten spies who surveyed the land. After hearing the news that giants consumed the territory they became terrified. Even worse, how they saw the giants didn't matter; it was how they viewed themselves that made the difference. They thought of themselves as grasshoppers.

As a man thinketh in his heart,
so is he. (Proverbs 23:7)

Principle thinking Christians live by the belief that God is greater than any problem. Therefore, they know all things are possible when God is in the plan.

Here's a principle that will serve you well to remember: If you don't live for something, you will fall for anything. You are not what you think you are, but what you think—you are. If you meditate on a negative image of yourself long enough you will begin to act on that image. However, if you are going to be what God would have you to be, you must see yourself the way God sees you.

God wanted to make Israel hell-stompers to remove all nations who failed to follow His ways. Yet, they chose to be grasshoppers jumping out of the way of the enemy. In order for God to move in our lives in a supernatural way, we must think according to His principles. If we're not principle thinkers we become susceptible to thinking only about our problems. Magnifying our problems can prevent God from doing what He wants to in our lives. Just as God could not bring that generation into the Promised Land, if we have unbelief, He will not bring us into our promised life.

Take heed, brethren, lest there be in any of
you an evil heart of unbelief, in departing
from the living God. (Hebrews 3:12)

The Achilles heel to principle thinking is having an evil heart of unbelief. The person with principle thinking believes in God's ability. The person with an evil heart of unbelief doubts God's ability and eventually turns from following the Lord.

Joshua and Caleb were principle thinkers. Thus, they saw God bigger and better than the giants. When we become principle thinkers we know Jesus is better than the life we lived before we knew Him. When times get hard the devil will paint pictures in your mind that life was better before you followed God. The devil is a liar! Whatever you do, don't stop following God. Resist the devil. When it's crunch time don't cringe. Live by the principle—my God is bigger, my God is better, my God is able to topple any opposition.

People who turn back from following God exhibit an evil heart of unbelief. They limit the Lord from revealing His power on their behalf. Having an evil heart is not the same as having a wicked heart. The person with a wicked heart fails to allow Jesus to change their heart. On the other hand, the individual with an evil heart is saved by faith, but fail to live by the faith they are saved by.

To better comprehend an evil heart we must consider the word evil. Evil is actually live spelled backwards. Thus, the revelation of the word is a backward life. Living backwards connotes living without God; leaving God out of the equation of your problem. Anyone who lives without God, the Lord calls evil hearted.

Attitude determines altitude. How high you go with God depends on the attitude you have towards Him. Your outlook determines your outcome. Many people experience the wrong outcome because they live by the wrong principle. Their principle for life is "I'll believe it when I see it." That's the wrong principle to govern your life. People who say I'll believe it when I see it almost never see it. When the time comes and they do get to see what they were looking for someone else is experiencing it in their life. When you tell God, "I'll believe it when I see it," He responds, "You'll see it when you believe it."

When people lack the principle thinking of God's supremacy and they're confronted with problems, they change lanes. They switch from being in the positive lane to traveling in the negative lane. All it takes to switch from positive to negative is complaining. Do not complain when adverse circumstances occur. Rather, train your heart to believe God. Teach your mouth to speak only what He has promised. And, transform your mind to think positively, ponder possibilities and practice God's principle.

If Israel would have stayed in the positive lane they could have arrived in the Promised Land in a matter of days. Instead, they murmured and complained their way into the negative lane. Their travel time expanded from several days to forty years. Even worse, after all that travel, all but two never possessed their inheritance. Two words caused them to forfeit God's promise—can God. Those in the negative lane will always ask, "Can God?" Albeit, commuters in the positive lane look for opportunities to declare, "God can!"

The people who say, "God can't!" will never experience His power to overcome. Yet, the people who declare, "God can!" will see His power and possess His promise. Decide now to possess your inheritance by staying in the positive lane. I'm in the positive lane as well, so when you see me smile and wave because we're doing better.

CHAPTER FOUR REFLECTIONS

The Lord is the _____ of our satisfaction and

the _____ for every problem we face.

In life it's so easy to get into the _____ lane.

We avoid unexpected exits in life by keeping our focus on our

_____ and staying in the _____ lane.

Staying in the positive lane consist of having _____,

_____ and _____ thinking.

Positive Thinking

_____ like gravity will pull you down.

The way of the world is _____ to the way of God.

Staying in the _____ lane keeps us on the right course.

Prosperity is the place for those who think _____.

When problems cause us to have a _____ attitude

we are conveying our unbelief in God.

Without the Lord many things can appear _____,

but with Him on your side all things become _____.

Possibility Thinking

_____ thinking prepares us to do better in life.

The words you speak come from what you _____.

Your belief comes from what you _____. How you think is based on your _____. There are only two sources from which we draw information, the _____ and _____.

True faith is not God getting you _____ of something; it's God walking you _____ something.

People who think " _____ _____ _____ _____ " have learned to wait on the Lord.

Without God the word is impossible, but with God it becomes _____.

Through faith all things are possible and we learn to lean on the Lord's_____.

Principle Thinking

To obtain God's kind of life would mean living by the Lord's _____ _____.

The Lord has one key principle in which all other principles rest

and that is _____ _____ _____.

_____ thinking Christians live by the belief

that God is greater than any problem.

Magnifying our _____ can limit God from what

He wants to do in our lives.

The Achilles heel to principle thinking is having an _____

_____ of _____.

Many people experience the wrong outcome because they live

by the wrong _____.

When you tell God, "I'll believe it when I see it." He responds,

"You'll see it when you _____ _____."

CHAPTER FIVE

HOW TO GET OVER SOMETHINGS

There is therefore now no condemnation to them which are in Christ Jesus, who walk not after the flesh, but after the Spirit. For the law of the Spirit of life in Christ Jesus hath made me free from the law of sin and death.
(Romans 8:1-2)

A VERSE IN THE BIBLE that has helped liberate my attitude in my Christian walk is John 10:10. This scripture reveals the thief comes with a single purpose—our demise. He utilizes the process of deception, division and ultimately destruction. The verse actually conveys he likes to steal, kill and destroy. Now, this is not the portion of the scripture that invigorates me.

After hearing how the devil wreaks havoc on us, my attention is won over by the Lord's purpose. The text says Jesus comes to give us abundant life. At this point, I would like you to understand something. Look at the verse and you'll notice that between the devil's purpose and Jesus' proclamation, there is a comma. So, I ask you, on which side of the comma do you want to live?

In our opening text (Rom. 8:1), there is a comma between the words "flesh" and "but." Again, what side of the comma will you reside? There is a right and wrong side and you must decide where you will be. Jesus is on the right side. Therefore, get over the comma and experience victory with the Lord.

VICTORY OVER CONDEMNATION

Although rather lengthy, I believe the following scriptures are important for us to read:

There is therefore now no condemnation to them which are in Christ Jesus, who walk not after the flesh, but after the Spirit. For the law of the Spirit of life in Christ Jesus hath made me free from the law of sin and death. For what the law could not do, in that it was weak through the flesh, God sending his own Son in the likeness of sinful flesh, and for sin, condemned sin in the flesh: That the righteousness of the law might be fulfilled in us, who walk not after the flesh, but after the Spirit. For they that are after the flesh do mind the things of the flesh; but they that are after the Spirit the things of the Spirit. For to be carnally minded is death; but to be spiritually minded is life and peace. Because the carnal mind is enmity against God: for it is not subject to the law of God, neither indeed can be. So then they that are in the flesh cannot please

God. But ye are not in the flesh, but in the Spirit, if so be
that the Spirit of God dwell in you. Now if any man have
not the Spirit of Christ, he is none of his. (Romans 8:1-9)

The Apostle Paul had a phenomenal way of writing. He wrote these verses strategically. He mentions the word flesh nine times and he references the word Spirit nine times. This is not by coincidence. Every time the flesh appears God's Spirit appears.

The term flesh in this context is the Greek word *sarx* meaning the body. This implies human nature with all its frailties. The flesh denotes our physical and moral passion. When we receive Jesus as Lord over our lives our spirits are saved instantly, our souls are saved progressively, but our bodies must still be placed under subjection.

Many people are still struggling with such issues as gluttony, pornography, anger, drunkenness to name a few. These are all works of the flesh and without a proper understanding; these carnal acts can leave us in a state of condemnation.

The question becomes, how do we avoid condemnation? Well, we circumvent condemnation by allowing God's Spirit to guide us. I know facing our sins can be disturbing, but it's necessary if we are going to progress in God's kingdom. Through His Spirit God will correct, instruct and direct us.

When we walk according to the Spirit and not our fleshly appetites we experience no condemnation. In fact, we gain the victory over condemnation. Victory is not something we achieve as a goal, it is what we receive as a gift because of the One we believe to be our God. No Christian ever needs to be defeated because we live in Christ. Regardless of where we are or what state we are in, Jesus Christ gives us the victory.

Again, the Apostle Paul's writing style is quite impressive. As a theologian Paul wittingly wrote in the indicative and imperative mood. In essence, the Apostle would give us Jesus' doctrine and leave us with a duty. After understanding our Lord's doctrine (what He did for us) we should be compelled to render duty (what we do for Him).

Thus, our duty ushers in the solution to victory over condemnation. We gain the victory by pursuing Jesus! Jesus our Savior has come from heaven to offer help. He helps us through the principles we learn in the Bible. However, we should never attempt to use the principles of Christ in order to reach Him. No, through pursuing Jesus we allow His principles to work on us and become an outflow of our lives.

Listen, it's critical that we do not enter into idolatry. This can occur if we marry the principle and not the person of Christ. Consider the following scripture for further understanding.

> *O wretched man that I am! who shall deliver*
> *me from the body of this death? I thank God*
> *through Jesus Christ our Lord. So then with*
> *the mind I myself serve the law of God; but*
> *with the flesh the law of sin. (Roman 7:24-25)*

HOW TO GET OVER SOMETHINGS

When recounting the effects of this body, Paul considered himself a wretched man. It was only through keeping his mind on Jesus and serving God's law did Paul possess the victory over condemnation.

Any attempt to live without the influence of God's Spirit will lead to defeat. A defeated life is one dominated by the lust of the eyes, the lust of the flesh and the pride of life. People pursue possessions, lofty positions and whatever else makes them feel good. However, these external factors can never substitute for internal peace. Only when our minds are on Jesus Christ are we able to have peace on the inside.

Life is difficult without God's Spirit to direct our paths. The devil has set up ambushes to ensnare us. He has hurdles to obstruct our journey. The devil uses tactics like deception and division for our destruction, but with the help of God's Spirit we can get over these things.

VICTORY OVER THE DEVIL'S TACTICS

Satan has many tactics to manipulate people. However, as God's children we do not have to be ignorant of the devil's devices. A major ploy of the devil is deception. He schemes in the shadows and navigates in the night.

One of the devil's greatest tactics is to convince the world that he doesn't exist. While the world indulges in pleasure there's a snake in the grass. He's difficult to detect, but he's there. Jesus called the devil the father of lies. Satan hardly ever confronts people. He simply walks alongside them and uses the power of suggestion.

How do we expose this filthy enemy and his cohorts? The best way to uncover falsehood is by presenting the facts. The only way to expose a lie is by confronting it head-on with the truth. There's an anecdote that expresses this sentiment further.

One very hot summer day Mr. Truth decided to cool off by skinny dipping in the lake. He removed all his clothes and hung them over a tree branch before jumping in the water.

Mr. Lie approached the same area of the lake undetected. He noticed Mr. Truth enjoying his swim. Lie decided to play a prank on his rival, Truth. He removed all his clothes, and quickly put on Mr. Truth's garments. Then he slipped away before Mr. Truth realized it.

Moments later, Mr. Truth emerged from the lake only to discover his clothes had been stolen. And since Mr. Lie left his clothes behind, Truth knew where to look.

Mr. Truth walked all around town looking to confront Mr. Lie. Finally, someone stopped him and asked, "Mr. Truth, do you realize you're not wearing clothes?" His response was, "I would rather be known as the naked truth than to parade around as a lie." When we confront the devil with the truth of God's Word it renders him ineffective.

Another deception the devil uses is impression. In the world the devil is depicted as this red demon with a trident. He's quite horrifying with the power to take lives at a moment's notice. This depiction is inaccurate. The Bible records that on the day the angels reported to God, Satan was there to give an account of his whereabouts to God.

Did you catch that? The devil had to report to God. He told the Lord he was in the earth seeking whom he could destroy. The reason he had to seek is because he doesn't possess the power to simply take lives. He needs permission in order to wreak havoc on God's people. Beloved, if you knew the power you possessed; more importantly, the Source of your power, you could attack hell with an empty water pistol and the fire would be out by the time you arrived.

The devil does not possess the kind of power you may think he has. He certainly is not the monstrous menace you probably perceive him to be. Now make no mistake, the devil has powers and he's been around much longer than any of us. So we must beware and not be caught sleeping at our posts of observation. Nevertheless, when we are strong in God's Word and connect with our Lord in prayer, the devil is outmatched.

The Bible records there will be a time when the men who were deceived by Satan will have the opportunity to see him. Upon further review, they will look at the devil's stature and stand amazed. They won't believe how someone so insignificant could pull the wool over the eyes of so many people (Isa. 14:15-16).

All I'm saying is the devil is not the big bad wolf, and you're not one of the three little pigs. You are more like the hunter holding a high powered rifle with the devil in your line of fire. As long as you belong to God, you have the power to overcome any tactic the devil tries to throw your way. Follow God's Spirit. He knows where to find the devil. He took Jesus in the wilderness to defeat the devil and will do the same for you.

When Satan comes at you with deception it's for division. He wants to separate you from the Lord. This is the ploy he utilized on Eve. Satan spun one spurious tale after another about Eve's identity and God's divinity. Rather than staying connected to God by faith, Eve allowed herself to be deceived. She partook of forbidden fruit and passed it on to her husband Adam and he too disobeyed God.

Through deception the devil caused division between God and humanity. It's important to note the devil approached Eve in paradise. Centuries later, the devil would get an opportunity to face-off with Jesus. Only this time the battleground was not in paradise, it was in the wilderness. Jesus took the fight to the devil to show us we can do the same.

When you feel weak, that's when God's at His strongest. When you feel confused, the Lord has all the answers. When you are engulfed in darkness, look to God's Word for light. Through Christ Jesus you are an overcomer. Jesus warned that this world brings tribulations. Then He encouraged us not to worry because He has overcome the world. Jesus overcame every issue we will encounter, the greatest being death. We are in Jesus. Therefore, we can experience victory over the devil's tactics and any limitations of the flesh.

VICTORY OVER THE LIMITATIONS OF FLESH

Throughout the chapter I've been expressing the necessity to get over some things. Many of the things we need to hurdle pertain to the appetites derived from the flesh. It is our flesh that sets limitations on our development. Our flesh prohibits us from obtaining the promises of God.

It is the spirit that quickeneth; the flesh profiteth nothing: the words that I speak unto you, they are spirit, and they are life. (John 6:63)

God's Spirit inspires us to live beyond the limits. Jesus was seeking to inspire His disciples. He told them that He was the bread from heaven able to sustain them continuously. Well, the disciples heard Jesus' invitation to eat, but they listened in the flesh and not in the spirit. Thus, many of them stopped following Him. Jesus was using symbolism while they were thinking cannibalism.

Jesus knew who would catch what He was conveying in their spirit and which disciples would receive the message from a fleshly standpoint. This is how God determines who can walk with Him. When we walk with God it must be in the spirit because along the way the Lord may say somethings that appear offensive. He wants to see our ability to get over some things.

When many of the disciples broke fellowship with the Lord, Jesus turned His attention to His original twelve. He asked them if they would also desert Him because of offences. Before anyone else could answer, Peter said, "To whom else can we go? You have the words of eternal life."

Peter recognized something many of his contemporaries did not; when it comes to the game of life, God holds all the pieces. As God deals a deck of cards, He has all the aces. The Lord shakes the orbits like a snow globe for His amusement. He keeps the Atlantic, Pacific, Indian and Arctic oceans as His fish bowl. Like E. F. Hutton, when Jesus spoke people listened, but not everyone listened in the spirit. Yet, Peter did.

Peter was not a perfect man. He had his flaws just like the rest of us. However, Peter had a way of listening in the spirit and because of that he was not limited in his life.

On another occasion Jesus asked His disciples, "Who do people say I am?" The disciples began naming off a list of high profile individuals, but none of them were high enough. Then suddenly Peter interrupted their replies with an answer of his own. Peter told Jesus, "You are the Christ, the Son of the living God." To His answer Jesus erupted, "Peter you are blessed because your answer did not come from flesh; it came from

God the Father." Peter heard God in the spirit and was able to respond spiritually.

Subsequently, Peter encountered some life events without limits. On the day of Pentecost, Peter preached a sermon to people of various backgrounds, cultures and ethnicities. As he preached, the Spirit of God moved and around three thousand people received salvation. Those numbers would make any preacher's mouth drop.

Then there was the time when the disciples found themselves stuck in a boat in the middle of rough waters. Jesus came walking across the water toward the disciples and they began ducking in fear, all of them except Peter. Peter shouted to the Lord to allow him to do the impossible—walk on the water. The Lord extended Peter the invitation to stroll on the water and Peter obeyed with alacrity.

Someone might say, "But didn't Peter eventually doubt God and begin to sink?" Yes, he had a momentary lack of faith, but he will forever be remembered as walking on water. Here's a good lesson; many times it's better to try and fail than to fail at ever trying. When you operate in the spirit and not your flesh, the limitations are removed and God's blessings are able to overtake you.

Faith inspires us to live beyond the limits. Faith will cause you to go where you would not normally go, believe what you do not see, give what you do not have and say what you do not feel. You can only do these things by the Lord's spirit.

When you operate according to the Spirit you will experience the unexplainable, reach the unattainable and receive the unpredictable. This kind of phenomenon will only be acquired by the Spirit. So, the next time you're facing unbelievable odds, get out of the flesh and get in the Spirit. Then the unbelievable becomes achievable.

Life brings with it certain difficulties. The obstacles you face are not to hinder you, but to help in your Christian development. No matter what it looks like, do not turn around. Resist the temptation to quit. Gaining the victory in life means you will have to learn how to get over some things.

When the devil tries to bring condemnation—get over it. Every time the adversary devises one of his tactics—get over it. When you sense limitations—get over it. When life brings the bitter—get over it and do better.

CHAPTER FIVE REFLECTIONS

The devil looks to bring our demise through the process of _____

_____, _____ and ultimately

_____.

Victory over Condemnation

The flesh denotes our _____ and _____

_____ passion.

When we receive Jesus as Lord over our lives our spirits are saved

_____, our souls are saved _____,

but our bodies must still be placed under _____.

Well, we circumvent _____ by allowing God's

Spirit to guide us.

Through His Spirit God will _____, _____ and

_____ us.

Victory is not something we _____ as a goal,

it is what we _____ as a gift because of the One we

_____ to be our God.

Regardless of where we are or what state we are in, Jesus Christ

gives us the _____.

We gain the victory by pursuing _____!

Idolatry can occur if we marry the _____ and

not the _____ of Christ.

A defeated life is one dominated by:

    1. _____

    2. _____

    3. _____

Victory over the Devil's Tactics

A major ploy of the devil is _____.

Jesus called the devil the father of _____.

Satan hardly ever confronts people. He simply walks alongside

them and uses the power of _____.

Another deception the devil uses is _____.

When Satan comes at you with deception it's for _____

_____.

Victory over the Limitations of Flesh

Many of the things we need to hurdle pertain to the appetites

derived from the _____.

Our flesh sets limitations on our _____.

God's Spirit inspires us to live beyond the _____.

Here's a good lesson; many times it's better to try and _____

_____ than to _____ at ever trying.

_____ inspires us to live beyond the limits.

Gaining the _____ in life means you will have

to learn how to get over some things.

CHAPTER SIX

THINK FOR A CHANGE

*Finally, brethren, whatsoever things are true,
whatsoever things are honest, whatsoever things
are just, whatsoever things are pure, whatsoever
things are lovely, whatsoever things are of good
report; if there be any virtue, and if there be any
praise,* **think on these things***.*
(Philippians 4:8 Bold Added)

THE GREATEST GAP between a person's success and
their failure is their capacity to think. Mark it down, many
people fail in life as a result of their thinking or dare I say, the
lack thereof. On the other hand, the people who succeed think
positively. There can be no positive thinking without exercising
faith.

Everyone uses faith. Some people place their faith
in their physicians, others in their government officials.
Yet, as Christians our faith is in the living God. Faith can

change facts and faith lives off the promises of God. Our promised life is packaged in Jesus. Everything we need and desire is in Him. In Jesus we live, move and have our being (Acts 17:28).

Paul enunciated a list of things we should think about in Philippians 4:8. We need to think on Jesus because it's all about Him. When we have our mind on Christ we will think of things that are true, honest, just, pure, lovely, of good reports, and things of virtue and praise.

Zig Ziglar said, "We need a check-up from the neck up" because some of our thinking is stinking. It is possible to have a heart that believes God and a head that is messed-up concerning the affairs of life. Jesus instructed His followers not to think about what they would wear, how they would eat or where they would live. As difficult as it may seem not to think on critical issues like the ones Jesus named, it's possible to do.

Instead of pondering the problems in life, we should focus on the Answer for life—Jesus. The Scripture reveals that success is accomplished by "looking" to Jesus (Heb. 12:2). Now, it didn't say look to Jesus, the command implies a continual looking to Jesus. This means we must never take our eyes off the Lord, but to place our focus and faith in Him. The verse then tells us why we continue looking at Jesus because He's the Author and Finisher of our faith. This means the Lord will work out our problems to completion.

Therefore, the objective of the Christian life is to adjust our thoughts to God and adopt His kingdom mindset. In short, this means we must think for a change.

THINK BETTER

*When he realized what he was doing, he thought,
'All of my father's servants have plenty of
food. But I am here, almost dying with hunger.
I will leave and return to my father and say
to him, "Father, I have sinned against God
and against you. . ." (Luke 15:17-18 NCV)*

There was a wealthy man who had two sons. The oldest son fancied himself the strong silent type. He prided himself on being there when his father needed him. However, he had a mean disposition. Then there was the younger son. He wanted more out of life than he thought he would find being at home with his father.

So, the young man decided to strike it out on his own. He wanted to discover what life had to offer, but he needed his father to pay for his education. Therefore, he approached his father requesting all of his inheritance. The father obliged his request while also giving his older son his inheritance as well.

The young man relocated and it wasn't long before he connected with some friends. He and his associates used up his money on superficial pleasures. They splurged and had everything in abundance. The son made no investments with his income he merely squandered it on foolish pursuits. His wasteful behavior continued until his resources dried up.

The young man looked around and discovered just as his money had vanished, so had his friends. No one stuck around in the hard times. There was no one he could count on for emotional, financial or spiritual support. As time progressed the young man's fortune worsened to the point he had no place to live and nothing to eat.

Finally, he found himself hitting rock bottom. In fact, he was under the rock. He resided in a foreign land with no family or friends to draw comfort. He did not respect the wealth he was given nor did he appreciate his father's love. Those mistakes would cost him everything right down to his dignity.

Now living the life of a vagabond, the young man had to beg for odd jobs. Even worse, he resorted to eating in strange places. This fellow had fallen to eating slop with the hogs in the pin. His bad decision had brought him from the palace to the pig's pin. He had every reason to fall into depression. Who would blame him? However, instead of sulking over his wrong moves, he adopted the right mind-set. In other words, in the midst of so much bad, he decided to think better.

Growing up he thought the world had much more to offer him than his father. He couldn't wait to become a man within his own right. He was fixated with the notion of coming out from under his father's shadow. Conversely, once he saw life in reality, he discovered something profound. He rose out of the hog's slop and said to himself, "I had it better in my father's house."

Once he thought better he made the choice to do better. In essence, he repented. To repent means you change your mind. But, it goes further than simply changing your mind. Repent is to change your mind and align it to the mind of Christ. When you think like God you're thinking better than you ever have thought before.

The young man thought the grass was greener outside his father's domain. It wasn't until he went through hardship that he realized it was better with his father than without him.

The young man walked back to his father's house rehearsing what he would say to win his dad's good graces. Once he was within eyeshot of the house, the wayward son received an immense surprise. The father couldn't wait for his son to reach the house so he ran to his boy. The father didn't give his son a lecture on behavior neither did he admonish him with disappointment. The wise old man greeted him with a hug, a kiss and extravagant gifts.

You may think your behavior has placed you on the Father's black list. If you do, think again. The Lord loves you and longs to embrace you with His forgiveness. To receive it you only need to think better. Thinking better positions you and sets you in a place to think bigger.

THINK BIGGER

Elisha said, "Take the arrows." So Jehoash
took them. Then Elisha said to him, "Strike the
ground." So Jehoash struck the ground three times
and stopped. The man of God was angry with him.
"You should have struck five or six times!" Elisha
said. "Then you would have struck Aram until
you had completely destroyed it. But now you will
defeat it only three times." (2 Kings 13:18-19 NCV)

Elisha lived a full life and worked twice as many miracles
as his predecessor. He had become sick and his illness would
be the cause of his death. Yet, before Elisha died he was visited
by the king of Israel. Elisha was faithful to his country and the
Lord had revealed Israel's critical fate to him.

So, before his death, Elisha gave the king instructions that
would empower Israel over their enemies. Elisha gave the king
an object lesson that would require the king's act of faith. The
prophet instructed the monarch to shoot an arrow out of the
window. The king shot the arrow and received a pronounced
blessing.

Next, Elisha told the king to strike the ground with his
arrows. The king did as he was instructed, but he struck the
ground three times only and stopped. His actions angered
Elisha. The prophet told the king had you struck the ground five
or six times you would have annihilated your enemy completely.

However, due to a lack of faith Israel's victory would be short lived.

Elisha wanted the king of Israel to think bigger than he was thinking. The king performed the action of striking the ground to simply go through the motion. The problem with simply going through the motion is you may come short of the mission. Elisha died after giving the king a stern rebuke.

When God tells you to do something don't just give Him a perfunctory effort. Give the Lord your best or don't give Him anything at all. When it's time to praise, God wants your best praise. When the time calls for a dance, try to dance out of your shoes. Whatever you do for God should be with no hesitation or reservation.

> *Clear lots of ground for your tents! Make*
> *your tents large. Spread out! Think big!*
> *Use plenty of rope, drive the tent pegs deep.*
> *You're going to need lots of elbow room for*
> *your growing family. (Isaiah 54:2-3 MSG)*

Wherever you are right now, it's not the end of your story. The Lord wants to enlarge your capacity to dream. What's keeping a lot of people from having the best is their inability to think on the best level. Can you see yourself doing better or having more than you've ever had in your life? I'm not talking about having an attitude of greed, but receiving the resources to go beyond sustaining just your family.

I can recall a time before my wife and I were married. We were spending some time in the downtown district of our hometown of Philadelphia, PA. On a brisk evening while taking a stroll together, we passed the front of this five star hotel. Neither one of us had the kind of money to spend the night in a place like that, but something came over me.

I told Valerie that I was going to enter that hotel just to see the inside of it. She protested at first. Valerie argued there was no reason for us to step into an extravagant establishment without the financial means to enjoy ourselves. Although I didn't have the money to spend in a place like that, I thought differently. Simply stated, I thought bigger.

Where I grew up we had a saying, "Don't have champagne taste on beer money." This meant you should not try to live beyond your means. Neither my wife nor I ever had that problem. I'm not promoting spending more money than you have or living where you can't afford. That would not be faith, that's considered foolishness. I'm talking about trusting God to take you higher, stretching you further and blessing you in a bigger way.

Valerie and I went into that five star hotel and it did wonders for our psyche. We got the opportunity to see how wealthy people enjoyed themselves. After perusing the place, I walked to the front desk and asked the clerk what it cost to receive a room for the night. Now, I cannot remember the amount of the room, but I do recall that his answer caused our heads to spin.

Even still, at that moment we determined one day we would be able to stay in a place like that one.

Call it window shopping; call it wishful thinking; but, I call it faith in God. We must think big because we serve a big God. He owns cattle on a thousand hills, the silver and gold belong to Him. Above all, this entire world is His and everything in it. God will not allow your mind to conceive what you physically cannot achieve. So, if you believe bigger you will receive bigger.

Thinking better leads to thinking bigger and ultimately, thinking brighter.

THINK BRIGHTER

The Lord wants us to think brighter. Just because we live in dark times doesn't mean we should allow our minds to be engulfed in darkness. We think brighter when we read the Bible. This is what God's Word accomplishes; it applies light where there would otherwise be utter darkness.

The very first experience we are exposed to in the Bible is the power of God's word. The Lord created our world to facilitate the needs of humanity. However, events occurred which prohibited the planet from cultivating life. The world became void and morphed into a black abyss. To remedy the defect, God spoke to night and commanded, "Let there be light!"

When the period projected dimness God did not sulk in disappointment. No, He allowed His mind to think brighter.

God is about making things brighter. He set the stars in their place. He created the sun for the daytime and even provided the moonlight for the night hours. That's important to know because there should never be a time when you have no light.

Think about this, the week begins on Sunday and when the sun sets, the evening is called Sunday night. Did you catch it? Even at nightfall it's call SunDAY night; day still takes precedence over night even when it's dark. So, when it appears darkness has befallen you, do what God did, command there to be light.

You cannot command light into a situation without thinking brighter. Darkness represents ignorance. When you are challenged on what to do or where to go; don't try to figure out what only God can work out. Whatever solution you need can be found in the Bible. Read God's Word daily and discover the answer you need to live a whole and healthy life.

When you need a way to feed your family, do not panic just think brighter. When there's money needed to provide for the children's education, rather than becoming frantic, think brighter. If a family member needs medical treatment and your health care is inadequate, think brighter. In every scenario as things get tight—think bright.

We cannot rely on the world to brighten our condition. The method of the world's system is designed to keep us in a perpetual state of panic. The world news constantly feeds us one negative report after another. We live in a Chicken Little world that's always crying, "The sky is falling!"

Truthfully, the people who do not know Jesus have every reason to worry. However, the child of God does not have to remain in the dark about social conditions. Even in the midst of darkness God has given us the resources to think brighter. We have His Word that provides light for our path. Also, we have His Spirit within us to enlighten us inwardly.

The scriptures tell us that Egypt was in complete darkness and at the same time God's people had light in the land of Goshen. And, when the time came for Israel to leave the region altogether they were pursued by their Egyptian oppressors. While fleeing the Egyptians, God caused there to be light for His people and darkness for their predators. The Lord will always provide light for His people; we just need to do our part by thinking brighter.

Jesus knew this world was a dark dismal place. Therefore, He came as the Bright Morning Star. His teachings were not received by all people. However, the ones who heard, listened and followed Him were given a specific assignment. The Lord told us to be lights on a hill to a world that's in desperate need of illumination.

It's impossible to provide light for others when our minds are darkened with depression. We have to receive the teachings of our Lord and allow them to shine for the sake of the people around us. Yet, we need to understand we are to be headlights and not spotlights. A spotlight is used to place the focus on a particular person or object.

Many Christians find fault in other people and place a spotlight of judgment on them. This is not wise because rather than drawing them to God, the sinner will run from God. On the other hand, a headlight illuminates the path allowing for safe passage. As headlights, we become the examples of how to behave and more importantly, how to believe in God.

Thinking brighter also involves seeing the bigger picture. When other people complain about the state of the world or the next crisis, they do so from a microcosm prospective. Thinking negatively causes us to examine our situation and arrive at a hopeless conclusion. But when we think brighter we see the world from God's perspective. Doing so allows us to enlarge the picture. We serve a big God and there's no problem he cannot solve.

Jesus told us to take no thought. Yet, He did not say, "Do not think." He did not want us to think negatively about life's conditions. However, seeing the big picture, in every situation we can think better, bigger and brighter. So, whenever you need to see your circumstances shift from bad to good—think, "I'm doing better."

CHAPTER SIX REFLECTIONS

The greatest gap between a person's success and their failure is

their capacity to _____.

On the other hand, the people who succeed think _____.

There can be no positive thinking without exercising _____.

Our promised life is packaged in _____.

When we have our mind on Christ we will think of things that are

_____, _____, _____, _____, _____,

of _____ reports, and things of _____ and

_____.

Zig Ziglar said, "We need a check-up from the neck up" because

some of our thinking is _____.

The objective of the Christian life is to adjust our _____

to God and adopt His _____ mindset.

Think Better

To repent means you change your _____.

Repent is to change your mind and align it to the mind of _____

_____.

When you think like God you're thinking _____

than you ever have thought before.

The Lord loves you and longs to embrace you with His forgive-

ness. To receive it you only need to think _____.

Thinking better positions you and sets you in a place to think

_____.

Think Bigger

The problem with simply going through the motion is you may

come short of the _____.

Whatever you do for God should be with no _____

or _____.

The Lord wants to _____ your capacity to

dream.

Trust God to take you _____, stretch you

_____ and bless you in a _____ way.

We must think _____ because we serve a _____ God.

God will not allow your mind to _____ what you

physically cannot _____ . So, if you believe _____

_____ you will receive _____ .

Thinking better leads to thinking bigger and ultimately, thinking

_____ .

Think Brighter

We think brighter when we read the _____ .

God is about making things _____ . He set

the _____ in their place. He created the

_____ for the daytime and even provided the

_____ for the night hours.

_____ represents ignorance.

In every scenario as things get tight—think _____ .

We have God's _____ that provides light for our

path. Also, we have His _____ within us to enlighten

us inwardly.

We need to understand we are to be _____ lights

and not _____ lights.

SOME THINGS DON'T COME EASY

THERE ARE THINGS that won't come easy in life. This does not mean God has not given it to you. It is no indication God does not desire for you to have it. Possessing some things will take every bit of your spiritual fiber. The reason for the difficulty is the Lord wants to see how bad you want it.

Receiving some things especially the better things in life will take a sacrifice. A little boy had made a tiny boat from some pieces of wood. He carved his name in the boat and started playing with it on a neighborhood lake. Suddenly, a gust of wind blew his boat further out into the lake. The boat was out of reach and soon beyond the boy's sight. The little boy had no way to retrieve his boat and was heartbroken about the ordeal.

Some weeks later, the little boy was passing a gift shop when he noticed what appeared to be his boat in the window. He rushed into the store and asked the store clerk to show him the boat. Upon inspection he discovered the boat was indeed his long lost treasure.

Now, the boat was a new color and had some other features that he did not give it. However, the boy saw his name still on the bottom of the toy. So, he asked the clerk if he could have his boat back. The clerk replied, "Not without a price." The store owner had paid for the boat and wanted compensation for his trouble.

The boy left the store with a promise to return with full payment for his boat. The boy did odd jobs for his neighbors just to earn enough money. Soon the lad returned to the store to purchase his boat. After giving the clerk the money he walked out of the store with a huge grin on his face.

The boy looked at his boat and was heard to say aloud, "Little boat, I love you because I made you and now I love you twice as much because I lost you, found you and paid to get you back." That's what the Lord did for us. He created us, lost us and paid to get us back. Why did God go through all the trouble to redeem us? Well, it's because He knows, some things don't come easy. And, when we discover the same we'll allow the Lord to usher us through darkness, danger and difficulty.

THE LORD IS MY LIGHT IN DARKNESS

People become very fearful in the dark. When you think about it, there's only one difference between an area that's lighted and then darkened—vision. We can see in the light what we are unable to see in the dark.

Personally, I am not afraid of the dark because the Lord is my light in darkness. I have learned to trust what the Lord sees. God sees things we do not see. When we face tough times or when we are given negative reports, we look to God for the answers.

As a pastor of a large church I am confronted with issues every day. Add to pastoring, I am a bishop over hundreds of churches throughout the world. So, the chance of becoming overwhelmed heightens in my line of work. Then consider I have in my employment over a hundred great people. Having all these people under my care can cause great stress.

As I wear the hats of pastor, bishop, and employer, I've learned the secret to success without stress. When dark clouds pass over my head I look up beyond the clouds. I seek the Lord above the clouds and say, "Lord you have a problem." The Lord tells us to cast our cares on Him because He cares for us. Yet, so many people take on the task of carrying burdens. I ask, "Why grope in the dark when the Lord provides light for darkness?"

Too many of God's people are living in the world with no hope. They allow the media to cast a dismal message. We hear the world's economy is in shambles; the state of unemployment is on the rise and health care is unaffordable. Receiving negative reports such as these can create gloom that many aren't able to overcome. For that reason, the Lord sends us (His people) to provide light to a world engulfed in darkness.

We are empowered and illuminated through prayer and God's Word. The Bible declares that the Lord lights every man that comes in the world" (Jhn. 1:9). The light we possess comes from Jesus residing in our hearts. When Jesus is left out of our lives, our only recourse is to stumble, fumble and grope our way to the ultimate darkness—death.

Death is considered dark because it's centered on the unknown. However, the child of God need not fear death. Death was an enemy, but now it's become our doorway from this world to God's heavenly state. The Bible says the last enemy that will be destroyed is death (1 Cor. 15:26).

Jesus took the sting out of death for the people of God. The apostle Paul asked, "Oh death where is thy sting? Oh grave where is your victory?" (1 Cor. 15:55). A Believer's death is described as "going to sleep." When the Believer wakes up they see Jesus. The curtains are drawn back and we see God's light on the other side of death's darkness.

A mother took her son and daughter to the park for a family outing. While playing the boy was stung by a bee. As he yelled in pain his mother attended to his wound. Then suddenly the little girl began to scream. The mother asked her, "Why are you crying?" The girl replied, "Because the bee is still buzzing around."

The mother then calmed her daughter and explained that the bee was buzzing, but was no longer a threat. She further explained how the bee had left its stinger in her brother.

This is what Jesus did for us. He took death's blow and survived death's bite. And, He did more than survive death; He defeated death so that we won't have to fear dying. Jesus blazed a trail for all of us to follow.

The Bible records a faithful follower of Christ named Stephen (Acts 7:54-60). This man became a martyr for God. He was persecuted and sentenced to death for his faith. As the hostile crowd stoned this man of God, he turned his attention from his tormentors and placed his focus on the Lord.

The bible describes Jesus as being seated by God. However, the day Stephen was stoned, Jesus stood up. In his darkest moment Stephen drew courage because the Lord became his light.

Many of the houses on the east coast have cellars. My grandmother's house in particular had a trap door on the front porch. This door led to the basement of the house.

Well, allow me to share an account of a man and his son. The man was storing his porch furniture in the basement using the same kind of trap door as my grandmother's.

While the man was in the basement his son stood on the porch. Suddenly, a blackout occurred. The boy panicked and began yelling for his father. The father stood in the basement looking up into the entrance. The moonlit sky provided enough illumination that the father could see his son's silhouette. However, the basement had no light so the son was unable to see his father.

The little boy started crying. He yelled, "Daddy, I'm afraid!" His Daddy said, "Son, don't be afraid." But the boy continued, "Daddy I can't see you!" The father explained, "Son, don't be afraid. Just take a step and you will fall right into my arms." Again, the child complained, "Daddy, I'm afraid. I cannot see you!" The father replied, "Son you don't need to be afraid, I can see you, take the step." Finally, the boy trusted his father, took the step into the trap door's entrance and fell safely into his father's arms.

We cannot see God, but God can see us. Therefore, He's telling us to take the step of faith. When times are dark and we cannot see, it's not always easy, but we must trust the Lord. He will direct us with His night vision.

I will instruct thee and teach thee in the
way which thou shalt go: I will guide
thee with mine eye. (Psalm 32:8)

The Lord will be our light to provide sight. I recall during childhood playing a game of "Blindfold." Someone would get blindfolded while another kid would bark commands. The blindfolded kid would listen carefully as instructions were given. When it was my turn to blindfold one of my friends I would play a prank on them.

"Take three steps forward. Then turn left. Take six steps," these were instructions I'd give. When I thought my friend was comfortable with my commands, I would give instructions leading him to stumble over something. Man I tell you, I would laugh and of course my friend would be upset. But, I thought it was worth it to get a good laugh.

Unlike my childhood antics, God does not lead us to make us fall, but to help us grow. His instructions are given for guidance and protection. The Lord will never prank us or lead us somewhere to cause us to stumble. We can trust God to be our light in darkness and our salvation in danger.

THE LORD IS MY SECURITY IN DOUBT

One of the benefits of being a child of God is we don't have to worry about a thing. It doesn't matter what circumstances appear, we can stare adversity in the face and confess, "I'm doing better."

The Lord is our security in times of doubt. When the economy plummets, while the rent is due and your funds depleted—don't doubt God. He knows you have needs and He sends the answer. Relief may not always arrive by your deadline because God is not operating on your timetable. The Lord created time so He's not subject to it. In fact, the Lord is not restricted in any sense.

Jesus had to minister to the crowds of people and so He sent His disciples ahead of Him. They rode by boat to their next destination. While on the sea, the weather took a turn for the worse. The boat tossed and bounced on angry waves. Just as the disciples grew anxious, they spotted what they thought was a ghost walking their way. They cried out in fear, but then a familiar voice spoke through all the panic. It was Jesus!

In all the hysteria Jesus brought hope. He told them to be cheerful and not afraid. How is that possible? When times are turbulent and your boat is rocking; how can you celebrate? You can smile in the storm because the Lord is your security.

Jesus knows everything. Therefore, when He sent them ahead in the boat, the bad weather was calculated in His travel plan. Understand when God gives you a plan for your business, family and future, He has already taken the forecast into consideration. So, when misfortune strikes don't doubt God, just look for Him because He's coming to your defense.

In all the commotion, Peter recognized the Lord. So he asked, "Lord if that's you allow me to come on the water." Now, that's strong faith. Peter was not asking to swim to Jesus; he requested to walk to Jesus. When you operate in faith not fear God permits you to do the unthinkable—incredible—even the impossible.

Some things don't come easy, but it doesn't mean they're not obtainable, it just means you have to grab them by faith. By faith Peter got out of the boat and started walking towards Jesus. Step-by-step-by-step he walked by faith. Then the

SOME THINGS DON'T COME EASY

elements became a factor. The winds became stronger; the waves increased and fear took the place of Peter's faith.

When you think about it, not many people would have gotten out of the boat. Just look at the other disciples and you'll see them cringing in the vessel as Peter tip-toed his way into God's history book. Did Peter eventually doubt God? Yes. Yet, that's not the end of the story.

As Peter took his eyes off Jesus and placed them on his scary surroundings, he began to sink. The water gave in and the super-natural became just the natural. However, before Peter could drown the Lord reached Peter, took His hand, and help His pupil. As Jesus pulled Peter from his sunken state He asked him, "Why did you doubt?" In essence, the Lord was conveying he was already doing the impossible—walking on water. Hence, why doubt the incredible when you're doing the impossible.

There's no need to fear the problems of tomorrow when you have received God's promise today. The Lord's promise is His security. He will not allow any of His promises to fall short of their goals. When God speaks a word He ensures that word will come to fruition. What has the Lord promised you? Are you still waiting for Him to perform it? If so, don't doubt what He has said because it will surely arrive on schedule. Understand, between the Lord's promise and performance there must be patience. Just remember, the promise will not necessarily come according to your plan; but will arrive at the exact time it is supposed to arrive. God's chronometer is not the same as yours. So, be patient and know you have security in His Word.

THE LORD IS MY STRENGTH IN DIFFICULTY

The Lord gives us strength for life's journey. In life we will become weary and in some cases we might contemplate giving up. When those moments occur, I encourage you don't give up; look up. The Lord strengthens us in times of difficulty.

We are living in troublesome times. Our nation has been facing challenges on both domestic and foreign fronts. In recent years, many of our communities have been pulled apart by poverty. As many people look to politicians for answers the phrase "empowering our communities" is often spoken, but rarely seen. Now, we should hold our government accountable, but our ultimate strength will not come from the White House but the "Power House."

The source of all power is God. It doesn't matter how much money the government or anyone else pours into our communities. Without the Lord's strength, we will not make it on life's journey with our peace intact. When we reject God's power we ultimately find ourselves disappointed, deflated and defeated. Albeit, when we obey God's instructions and abide by His directions, we will experience victory.

Victory is not something we achieve as a goal; it is something we receive as a gift because of the Someone we believe to be our God. Joshua and the children of Israel learned this first hand. On their journey to their promised land they encountered many enemies. Jericho proved to be a formidable opponent. This city's toughness was not its warriors, but its walls.

God's plan was not for Israel to go around Jericho, but to go through it. Jericho placed their trust in their fortress, but Israel had the ultimate Ace up their sleeves—God. The Lord met with Joshua and gave this general the rules of engagement. God's instructions did not involve weapons of mass destruction. The plan did not even call for Israel's armed forces. The Lord told Joshua to command the nation of Israel to do just two things; keep walking and keep silent. That's it!

Israel did not have to engage in any conversation with the enemy. They did not have to strategize or figure out logistics. God just gave them a tactical instruction—walk around the city.

Many times God's people feel overwhelmed by life. The duties and deadlines, schedules and social events can seem overwhelming. Nevertheless, the Lord doesn't want these things to surround us, so He commands us to surround them. God is telling us when we face problems—walk around them. And, when you walk don't say anything.

Too often when we face problems we speak in fear and not faith. We can look at our bills and say, "I don't have enough money." We can consider the doctor's report and conclude, "I don't have enough strength." We can confront multiple challenges and blurt out, "I don't have enough time." In all these cases, if we respond in the negative we have surrendered our God-given power.

The Lord wants us to walk around the issues we face until we are no longer intimidated by them. Like Joshua, meet with the Lord concerning the issues that confront you. And after you tell God about your problems, go and tell your problems about your God.

Israel did as the Lord commanded. They walked around Jericho in complete silence for seven days. On the seventh day, Israel let out a shout of praise for their God and the strength of the Lord was felt through their voices. Jericho's walls crumbled as God's strength was on display.

It's true, somethings don't come easy, but when you obey God many things will. The Lord will be your light in darkness, your security in doubt and your strength in difficulty. Give Him access to perform in these times of hardness. The result will leave you saying, "I'm doing better!"

CHAPTER SEVEN REFLECTIONS

Receiving some things especially the better things in life will take

a _____.

When we discover some things don't come easy, we'll allow the

Lord to usher us through _____ , _____

and _____.

The Lord is my Light in Darkness

People become very fearful in the _____.

Too many of God's people are living in the world with no _____

_____.

The Lord sends us (His people) to provide _____ to

a world engulfed in darkness.

We are empowered and illuminated through _____

and God's _____.

The Bible says the last enemy that will be destroyed is _____

_____ (1 Cor. 15:26).

A Believer's death is described as " _____ _____ _____."

The Lord will be our light to provide _____.

We can trust God to be our light in darkness and our salvation in

_____.

The Lord is my Security in Doubt

You can smile in the storm because the Lord is your _____

_____.

Understand when God gives you a plan for your business, family

and future, He has already taken the _____ into

consideration.

When you operate in faith not fear God permits you to do the

_____ — _____ —even the

_____.

The Lord's _____ is His security.

What has the Lord promised you? Write it here:

_____

_____

_____

_____

God's chronometer is not the same as yours. So, be patient and know you have security in His _____.

The Lord is my strength in Difficulty

The Lord gives us _____ for life's journey.

The source of all power is _____.

When we reject God's power we ultimately find ourselves

_____, _____ and _____.

Too often when we face problems we speak in _____

and not _____.

After you tell God about your _____, go and tell

your problems about your _____.

The Lord will be your light in _____, your security in

_____ and your strength in _____.

CHAPTER EIGHT

THE MAGNETISM OF OPTIMISM

MAGNETS ARE UNIQUE OBJECTS. They can either attract or repel each other. Magnets have this invisible force around them that's called a magnetic field. The magnetic field attracts material made of iron to it. As with magnets, God's people possess an invisible force that can either attract or repel objects and people. I call this phenomenon the Magnetism of Optimism.

God's people have an attraction deriving not from something, but Someone. The Source behind the force of the magnetism of optimism is Jesus. God created us to multiply and to produce fruit in our lives. Thus, He's given us the ability to fill places that are void. Another way to see the magnetism of optimism is by operating in Jesus Christ's anointing.

The Lord's anointing removes burdens and destroys yokes from our lives. God's anointing is His grace empowering us to perform at all levels of life. Someone could request that you dig a six foot hole in the ground. You could oblige their request by digging the hole with your hands or with a core drill rig. Digging it with your hands will require a lot of back-breaking work and time. Digging the hole with a core drill rig will be a lot easier and faster. The drill rig is God's grace, but acquiring such equipment depends on the magnetism of optimism.

THE KEY TO MAGNETISM

Jesus is the key to having God's magnetism of optimism. Therefore, to the degree we allow Jesus access to our lives we will experience positive results.

> *The Spirit of the Lord is upon me, because he*
> *hath anointed me to preach the gospel to the*
> *poor; he hath sent me to heal the brokenhearted,*
> *to preach deliverance to the captives, and*
> *recovering of sight to the blind, to set at liberty*
> *them that are bruised. (Luke 4:18 KJV)*

Have you ever wondered why so many people were attracted to Jesus? Wherever He went large crowds gathered to Him. It was because of the magnetic pull of His optimism. Jesus could not be hidden. Throughout His life, the magnetism of optimism was activated.

The key to Jesus' magnetism was He never sought glory for Himself. He would always give God the Father credit for everything good that happened in His life. In the previous scripture Jesus announced that He preached the gospel to the poor and was sent to heal the broken hearted. He declared deliverance to the captives, blind people regained their sight and He liberated people who were bruised. However, in every one of His exploits, Jesus announced He did it all with God's anointing.

There was no pronouncement of His birth. His parents could not even get a room in a decent hotel. In fact, they could not find any establishment that would accept them. Therefore, Jesus was born in a stable.

Even still, the day Jesus was born wise men notified King Herod. These men did not tell the king a baby came into the world they spoke of the King of the Jews coming forth. This troubled Herod so much that he sent the wise men to discover Jesus' whereabouts and beckoned them to return with the news.

The wise men set out on their search for the Lord and they had no trouble locating Him. Amazingly, there was a star which they first saw in the east that led them straight to Jesus. The sages followed the star until they were facing the Lord in person. Even as a child Jesus possessed the key to magnetism.

As Jesus got older and grew in strength, the time came for Him to be baptized. In those days John the Baptist preached in the wilderness. Many people of all classes and social backgrounds came to John to receive forgiveness for their sins. Once forgiven, they were baptized by him.

Now John was an impressive man in his own right. He lived a life minus material wealth. He chose to live in the wild and to focus on bringing people to a place of worship. However, John didn't teach people to worship through songs or music; his plan was for them to live a life that worshipped God. John had one message—repent (change your thinking).

John had a dynamic ministry, but he was never a substitute for Jesus, just his representative. God used John to prepare the path for Jesus' ministry. Every day John spent long hours converting people from a path of selfishness to selflessness.

People flocked to John's meetings, but only because he understood the key to magnetism. Just as Jesus pointed people to God the Father, John directed their attention to Jesus the Christ.

There's significance behind Jesus pointing to God and John to Jesus. The important factor we must not miss is how focusing on the Lord keeps us in the positive lane. Moving in the positive lane is the key to magnetism where we maintain gratitude in our attitude. Our attitude takes us to the altitude of operating in the God zone.

When we operate in the God zone, placing our faith in Jesus, our necessities are drawn to us. David wrote God's goodness and mercy will follow me all the days of my life," in the 23rd Psalm. Jesus affirms that the Father knows what we need (Matt. 6:32). Now, here's the key, Jesus instructs His listeners to seek God's kingdom and the necessities of life will be added to them.

Therefore, knowing God has our needs in mind we do not have to worry. We need to remain positive. People love being around positive people. There is so much negativity in this world that positivity seems to be a low commodity. When you maintain a positive perspective you can accomplish goals and acquire gains.

Both Jesus and John understood the key to magnetism stems from a focus on the Lord. By focusing on the Lord we consider His ability to unlock all possibilities. There are God-given goals that need to be completed, but many people put them off because of fear of failure. The Bible tells us to always look to Jesus because He is the Author and Finisher of our faith (Heb. 12:2). When we focus our attention on the Lord, failure becomes a nonfactor to our success.

LIVE UP IN A DOWN WORLD

Jesus took three of His disciples up into a high mountain (Matt. 17:1). Just as He took them, He desires to take us all—up. This world can be a tough place to live. In fact, the law of gravity describes the state of this world. Gravity is a force that naturally pulls downwardly. Even though this world consists of gravity the Lord is compelling us to live up in a down world.

Jesus took His disciple up and apart so when they came down they would not fall to pieces. How do you respond to negative news? Do you collapse when you hear of catastrophes or do you look up to God for solutions?

The children of Israel experienced a famine in their land because of their disobedient lifestyle. At the time, Ahab was their king. This monarch faced the difficulty of feeding his people, but only because he failed to follow God.

King Ahab sent Obadiah, the governor of his house, throughout the region, looking for favorable conditions. While seeking for a territory that was suitable Obadiah came across the prophet Elijah. Elijah was sent on a mission from God to get Israel's lifestyle back in agreement with God's law. In essence, Elijah came to remind them to live up in a down world.

King Ahab had eight hundred and fifty prophets who did evil in God's sight. These prophets were bad examples for Israel. Therefore, the Lord sent Elijah to clean house. Elijah called for a showdown between his God and the gods of the false prophets. Elijah chose the place for the confrontation, Mount Carmel.

This location held significance because it caused the entire nation to come up. They had been living below standards long enough. It was time for God to reintroduce Himself and He was not going to do it in the valley. The Lord wanted the people to head in an upward direction. Carmel in the Hebrew language means *Garden of God*. Thus, the Lord was going to use this place to plant His people firmly back into their faith in Him.

The confrontation began in the morning with the false prophets standing and doing their incantations. It concluded with their defeat, and all of Israel bowing in submission to the Most High God. Elijah told the people to choose to live for God or die for the false deities. In other words, he admonished them to live up in a down world.

We can only live up in a down world by choosing to live that way. The apostle Paul warns us not to be conformed to this world, but to be transformed by renewing our minds. Renewing our minds means we think on the things that pertain to godliness not worldliness. The Word of God instructs us to set our affections on things above not on things on the earth (Col. 3:2). Setting our affections on things above means being determined to live up in a down world.

After defeating King Ahab's false prophets, Elijah turned his attention to the king with a word from the Lord. He told Ahab where to find food and drink for the famished nation. Elijah directed the king to go up in order to receive an abundance of rain.

As the king obeyed God's prophet, Elijah fell to the ground and placed his head between his knees. This was his way of communicating with God despite surrounding distractions. Then, Elijah sent his servant up to discover God's rain for their drought. After some time, the servant returned with the report of no rain. So, Elijah instructed him to go up seven more times. On the seventh ascent the servant witnessed the move of God.

Elijah's servant looked toward the sea where he discovered the hand of God rising out of the water. The servant notified Elijah of the event and the prophet told him to go up and inform the king that the Lord was delivering their blessing. King Ahab received the word from the servant along with instructions to go and make preparations for God's people.

We can learn from Elijah's servant. The servant went up expecting to see a move from the Lord and nothing happened. So he returned to his master with a negative report. However, Elijah instructed him to go up and not give up.

Too often when we look for answers from the Lord, we want immediate results. When we do not see the desired effects according to our timetable we conclude the Lord is not doing anything. This is not the case. The Lord cares to do something in us more than He's concerned about doing something for us. Our seeking Him causes us to live up in a down world.

Like in the case with Jesus and His disciples, Ahab had to go up and apart so he could eventually come down and not fall to pieces. This is an example of doing better. We must possess the ability to hear and see God so we can live for Him when conditions are not favorable.

Elijah was able to bring Israel back under the protection of God because he had the magnetism of optimism. So, trust God and through the magnetism of optimism you can cause other people to live up in a down world.

DO GOOD IN A BAD WORLD

How God anointed Jesus of Nazareth with the
Holy Ghost and with power: who went about
doing good, and healing all that were oppressed
of the devil; for God was with him. (Acts 10:38)

Jesus is the ultimate example of doing good in a bad world. Right now grammarians are falling out of their seats. They complain, "Doing good is not proper English!" Well, it may not be proper English, but it's surely proper behavior. Besides, if the Bible says Jesus went about doing good then we ought to follow His example.

Jesus went through various regions for the purpose of healing the sick, delivering the demon possessed and doing other good works. There was a popular slogan in the late 90s that asked, "What would Jesus do?" I love that slogan, but would appreciate action even more. There's no need to ask, "What would Jesus do?" if we're not going to follow His example.

Whenever we do good for others we are operating with the magnetism of optimism. This doesn't mean that bad things will not occur; it simply means the bad things will not affect us in a negative way. Our dependency on the Lord allows us to strengthen the people around us.

There was an occasion when Jesus taught a Bible study in someone's house. The news spread that Jesus was in town and people from the neighboring cities brought their sick to Him for healing. One man in particular had a disease which caused him to be bedridden. This man did not possess the power to get to Jesus on his own, but he had friends who decided to do good in a bad situation.

The friends carried this man to the house where Jesus taught. However, there were so many people that they were unable to enter the house through the door. Yet, these friends were determined to get their ailing pal to Jesus. So, they decided to lift their sick friend with his bed to the rooftop.

They broke through the roof and lowered their companion to Jesus. The Lord was impressed by their faith. Their faith in God compelled them to good deeds. These men did not let the distance to Jesus stop them from carrying their friend. They did not allow the enormous crowd to deter them from finding a way of deliverance.

How far will you go to do good in a world that's bad? Will you allow distance to hinder you from bringing someone to Christ? Will you not come to hear a Word from the Lord because the church is too large?

We live in a sin, sick, secular society. The world around us is morally falling apart. Society's standards are decaying and sound principles are becoming nonexistent. God has not turned His back on the world; the world has turned its back on God. Nevertheless, people still need the Lord and are longing to discover His love.

God is looking for a Church that will take a stand in a falling world, be light in a dark world, live up in a down world and do good in a bad world. Will you heed the call of the Lord? Are you ready to blaze a trail for others to find Jesus?

There is a magnetism of optimism, but know there is a magnetism of pessimism as well. Evil and hurtful things come to those who are pessimistic. Job said, "The thing I greatly feared has come unto me" (Job 3:25). He pondered on pessimistic thoughts every day until his thoughts became his reality. Negativism draws whatever you fear to you. The Gospel is called the "The Good News" because God transforms negatives into positives.

Jesus Christ died (that's a negative) for our sins (that's a positive). He was then buried (that's a negative), but God raised Him on the third day (that's a positive). In this world we will have trouble (that's a negative), but Jesus overcame any problem we will face (that's a positive). Therefore, we do not have to focus on the negatives; we can fix our faith until we have the positives.

One particular year California experienced a terrible storm. The rainstorm destroyed all the grapes. Many farmers became discouraged because their grapes were smashed. One farmer decided to leave his grapes on the vine. When the sun came up and beat on those rotten and ruined grapes, they were transformed into plump juicy raisins. Thus, began the California raisin industry.

When we allow the *Son* to shine on our rotten ruined lives, God is able to take the negatives and turn them into positives. Whoever you are and whatever negative situation you may be facing, know God can transform your negative into a positive. Afterwards, you will be empowered to do good and bring positive energy into the lives of many people.

The magnetism of optimism is the energy that allows you to live up in a down world and do good in a bad world. So no matter the circumstances, declare today, "I'm doing better!"

CHAPTER EIGHT REFLECTIONS

Magnets have this invisible force around them that's called a

_____ _____ .

God's people possess an invisible force that can either attract or

repel objects and people. I call this phenomenon the _____

_____ _____ _____ .

The source behind the force of the magnetism of optimism is

_____ .

God's anointing is His _____ empowering us

to perform at all levels of life.

The Key to Magnetism

_____ is the key to having God's magnetism

of optimism.

The key to Jesus' magnetism was He never sought _____

_____ for Himself.

Moving in the positive lane is the key to magnetism where we

maintain _____ in our _____ .

People love being around _____ people.

By focusing on the Lord we consider His _____ to

unlock all _____.

Live Up in a Down World

Even though this world consists of gravity the Lord is compelling

us to live _____ in a _____ world.

Carmel in the Hebrew language means _____ _____

_____.

The Word of God instructs us to set our affections on things

_____ not on things on the _____ (Col. 3:2).

The Lord cares to do something _____ us more than He's

concerned about doing something _____ us.

Trust God and through the _____ _____ _____

_____ you can cause other people to live up in a down world.

Do Good in a Bad World

Jesus is the ultimate example of doing _____

in a bad world.

There's no need to ask, "_____ _____ _____

_____?" if we're not going to follow His example.

We live in a _____, _____, _____ society.

The world around us is falling apart _____.

God has not turned His back on the _____; the
world has turned its back on _____.

God is looking for a Church that will take a _____ in a falling
world, be _____ in a dark world, live _____ in a down
world and do _____ in a bad world.

_____ draws whatever you fear to you.

The Gospel is called the " _____ _____ _____ "
because God transforms negatives into positives.

CHAPTER NINE

THE BLESSEDNESS OF HAPPINESS

He went up into a mountain: and when he
was set, his disciples came unto him: And
he opened his mouth, and taught them,
saying, Blessed. . . (Matthew 5:1-3)

I DON'T KNOW HOW people live in this world without God. Try as you may, but it's impossible to find true happiness while eliminating Him. That may be the reason Jesus' first sermon was a teaching on happiness.

Jesus saw people (Matt. 5:1). That's important to know because many people are under the misbelief that God is aloof to their struggles and oblivious to their pain. This idea is totally off base. Jesus saw people and more importantly, He understood what they were going through.

Jesus came near individuals with a message that was needed for the problems they faced. Theologians have coined

His first sermon the "Beatitudes." The meaning behind the title is simple, Jesus declared let this *be* your *attitude*. Attitude is critical in determining how we progress in life. Success will rise or fall because of attitude.

Jesus gave His audience nine beatitudes. These beatitudes carry the connotation of blessings. Being blessed is a state of supreme happiness. Understand, the world's happiness differs from God's happiness. The world's happiness derives from an old Anglo-Saxon word, "happenstance." Happenstance is where we get the English word "circumstance." Hence, if things are happening the way you want them to happen, you are happy. However, if things don't go your way, you are unhappy.

We live in a cruel world filled with hate, hypocrisy and hurt. Nevertheless, Jesus came to bring happiness. As Christians, our happiness is rooted in our relationship with the Lord. So, Jesus asked His disciples, "Who do you say that I am?" Peter answered, "Thou art the Christ, the Son of the Living God." After hearing Peter's response Jesus declared, "Blessed art thou, Peter, because you know who I am, and upon this rock I will build my church" (Matthew 16:15-18). To the degree we know Jesus determines the blessedness of our happiness.

Our blessedness stems from our relationship with God. Our happiness derives from allowing the Lord to develop us. Collectively, we are called the Lord's Church. Since we are His, we must become a Triple "A" Church.

The Word of God emphatically states, *"Except the LORD build the house, they labor in vain that build it"* (Ps. 127:1). Jesus wants us blessed and happy. Therefore, He is strategically building His Triple "A" Church. This means we have an appreciation for God's Word, an affection for God's house and an aspiration for God's cause.

APPRECIATION FOR THE WORD OF GOD

Jesus Christ is the Word of God personified. Usually people don't think of God's Word and Jesus synonymously. Jesus is the truth (Jhn. 14:6). God's Word is the truth (Jhn. 17:17). Therefore, Jesus and the Word are one in the same. In fact, the Bible reveals everything was made by God's Word. Afterwards, God's Word took on the form of man and that man was Jesus (Jhn. 1:14).

Therefore, our appreciation for the Lord will reflect how we treat His Word. We need to know a casual usage of the Bible is not enough to maintain good success. The Lord instructed His people to meditate in His Word day and night. Obeying His instructions resulted in good success (Jos. 1:8). The same instructions apply to us today. As we receive God's correction, instruction and direction we will discover good success.

God can give you instructions and to the degree you follow His word will determine your success. Some people hear a word from the Lord and give Him partial obedience. Yet, it must be understood that partial obedience is disobedience.

Jonah was given instructions to deliver a message to the people of Nineveh. Now, these people were ruthless. They did not follow God nor did they have any respect for God's people or their way of living. The people of Nineveh were extreme terrorists who led by intimidation and fear. This ruthless nation had shown particular harshness to Israel. So, Jonah had developed a relentless prejudice toward them.

Jonah's prejudice for Nineveh got in the way of obeying God's word. Instead of going where the Lord instructed, Jonah boarded a ship headed in the opposite direction. It wasn't long before Jonah's disobedience brought extreme discomfort to him and the other passengers on the ship. God caused a perfect storm which almost destroyed the vessel.

When we fail to adhere to God's Word it places us at a disadvantage, but it can put the people around us in danger, also. Sometimes family members and friends suffer because of the stubbornness of God's servants.

So, the ship was being tossed and no one knew the reason for the sudden terrible weather. Well, no one knew except Jonah. Jonah understood the sudden storm was a result of his failure to follow God's word. However, rather than getting in agreement with God, Jonah decided to continue his own way.

Jonah asked the mariners to throw him overboard. This man would rather die than follow the plan of God. The mariners did their best to remove everything they thought would alleviate damage to the ship. Finally, when nothing else worked, they agreed to give Jonah his request. The men tossed Jonah overboard and before he could drown a fish swallowed him whole.

Jonah's condition went from bad to worse. He was now traveling under water inside a fish. Jonah's predicament is not uncommon when you think about it. I mean it is rather strange to find yourself in the belly of a fish. However, many of us have been in some tight situations as a result of not heeding God's Word.

Some people have received God's warning not to marry and fellowship with particular people, work in some places or live in certain states. Although the Lord gives His word not everyone obeys His word. These disobedient servants find themselves in tight situations. The question becomes, when you are in over your head and it appears the walls are closing in, what do you do?

When times are tight and things not right ask yourself, is it my doing that brought about my condition. It took Jonah days in that fish before he reached the point of submission. While deep in despair and even deeper in the fish, Jonah prayed for the Lord's salvation.

After admitting his wrong and seeking the Lord's help; God spoke to the fish. Now that's amazing, the Lord spoke to the fish and the sea monster obeyed. The fish vomited Jonah out on dry land. Then God sent His word again for Jonah to speak to the people of Nineveh. This time the prejudice preacher obeyed. Jonah learned to have an appreciation for God's word. He followed the Lord's instructions and the people of Nineveh heard and submitted to God.

We need an appreciation for the Word of God. Respect for God's Word ensures us of His presence and preservation. It's impossible to have an appreciation for God's Word without having affection for the Lord's house.

AFFECTION FOR THE HOUSE OF GOD

If you love the God of the house; then you have to love the house of God. David was compelled by His love for God. Therefore, He loved every opportunity to come into the house of God.

God said, *"David is a man after my own heart and he will fulfill all my will"* (1 Sam. 13:14; Acts 13:22). We discover in Psalm 122:1 David saying, "I was glad when they said unto me let us go into the house of the Lord." David was glad when approached about going to God's house. He didn't wait until he arrived at church before he expressed his delight.

There are things we love such as sports, entertainment, education, politics, etc. However, nothing should have preeminence over our love for God. And, a sure fire way we display our love for the Lord is how we treat His house.

David said, "O taste and see that the Lord is good" (Psalm 34:8). How we taste and see is by coming to see. We must come to the house of God with gladness not sadness, or dragging, sagging and lagging.

There must be a love for serving in the church with gratefulness. Serving the Lord with gratitude in your attitude takes acknowledging what the Lord has done for you. He made a way where there was no way. When we consider how the Lord has blessed us exceedingly, abundantly, above all we could ask or even think; it compels us to serve in His house.

David expressed, "I had rather be a doorkeeper in the house of my God" (Psalm 84:10). That's a wonderful and humbling sentiment. The Lord chose David to rule over Israel as king. Yet, David longed to be a doorkeeper in the house of God. Many times pastors try to get congregants to serve in God's house when they (the pastors) have trouble serving God.

I heard a funny little anecdote that comes to mind. One Sunday morning a mother yelled upstairs, "Johnny it's time to get up and go to church!" Johnny obviously disturbed by his mother's demand responded, "Oh mom, why do I have to go to church?" His mother yelled back at him, "Johnny, I'll give you two reasons why you have to go to church. First, you're fifty-five years old. Second, because you're the pastor!"

I love coming to church. Now, I understand a statement

like that coming from me can be easily misconstrued. Someone may think I love coming to church because I'm a pastor. It's true that as a pastor, I should not be like Johnny in the previous anecdote. Nevertheless, my wife and I loved coming to church before we became pastors.

Our testimonies are not without blemishes. We have not been saved all our lives. Personally, I have done some things worthy of jail and certainly hell. But God! The Lord has done so much for me, my wife, my family and the people He has trusted me to pastor. It causes me to have an appreciation for the house of God and His principles.

Jesus gave parables in order to teach kingdom principles. I consider Luke 15 the crowning jewel of all His teachings. This parable starts with a man that lost and found his sheep. After finding his precious animal, the man called his neighbors and friends to rejoice with him. Jesus then segued to another account of a woman.

This woman lost a piece of silver. One piece may seem insignificant, but she started with ten pieces. In biblical numerology ten is the number of completion. So, if she did not find the one piece her set would be incomplete. Therefore, she swept the house looking for the lost silver. Finally, she located the missing piece and called her friends and neighbors to rejoice with her. Furthering His point, Jesus discussed a man and his sons.

This man had two sons and both had lost their way. The

younger son demanded of his father, "Give me what is mine." The Father acquiesced to his son's demand. However, the father gave his younger son his inheritance early. Understand, the son had no right to any inheritance while the father still lived. Nevertheless, the father dispersed birthrights to both his sons.

The younger son left home and squandered all his money on friends and the fast life. After he lost everything he hit rock bottom. When it seemed things couldn't get worse, he was reduced to eating pig slop. It was at this point he came to himself.

The lost boy said to himself, "I had it better in my father's house." Thus, he discovered affection for his father's house. He fixed his heart and headed back to his Father's house. As he traveled home he prepared an apology. The words of his apology sounded like this, *"I've sinned against heaven and I've sinned against you. I am no longer worthy to be called your son. Make me a hired servant."*

The Father saw his youngest son walking toward the house afar off and ran to meet him. The father ran to his son for a couple of reasons. First, I'm sure he missed his child. Second, the Law of Moses stipulated if a child disrespected their parents they could be stoned to death. Ultimately, the father sought to protect his boy from would-be-persecutors.

The father kissed his son, put his best robe and ring on his boy and called for a feast in his honor. This account represents the love God has for you as His child. In all three accounts, something or someone was lost and then found. And in every scenario celebration ensued after recovering what was lost.

You may not always hit the mark or make the right decisions, but God will cover you. He will help you recover what you've lost and celebrate with you. Remember, have affection for God's house. When times get tough do not leave His house because He has a place at his table with your name on it. The Lord is a strong tower where His children can find refuge from the storms of life.

In life we will experience hard times, but we can rejoice. Our rejoicing is not about the conditions in life, but our position in Christ. Jesus had to endure suffering, but afterward He enjoyed the blessedness of happiness. He set an example for us to follow.

ASPIRATION FOR THE CAUSE OF GOD

There is a difference between inspiration and aspiration. Inspiration is something you feel on the inside. Aspiration is a desire, a longing. It's a quest for something higher in life. We must have an aspiration for the cause of God.

God's cause is higher than anything we could desire. To reach the purpose of God and fulfill His will means going through persecution. Anything worth having is worth fighting for. Many of God's people fall short of receiving His promise because they take the path of least resistance.

> *Blessed are ye, when men shall revile you, and persecute you, and shall say all manner of evil against you falsely, for my sake. Rejoice, and be exceeding glad: for great is your reward in heaven: for so persecuted they the prophets which were before you. (Matthew 5:11-12)*

Supreme happiness is not based on what's happening; it's based on who God is and the fulfillment of His cause. It's called the joy of the Lord. The joy of the Lord is where we draw our strength. Jesus gives nine beatitudes and he concludes, *"Blessed are they which are persecuted for righteousness' sake and blessed are you when men shall revile and persecute you* (Matt. 5:10a, 11a)."

The bible records, *"all that will live godly in Christ Jesus shall suffer persecution"* (2 Tim 3:12). There is no one who lives for God who will not be persecuted. On another occasion Jesus said, *"If the world hate you, you know that it hated me before it hated you"* (Jhn. 15:18).

When you believe in God and live for God you will receive wrong from the world. But God will reward you in the midst of it. He blesses you coming in and going out; in the city and in the field (Deut. 28:6). God wants you to experience the blessedness of happiness. This experience does not mean everything will happen the way you prefer. Nevertheless, praise God amidst trials, temptations and tribulations.

God has a people who will go through their passage of pain and disappointment. Listen, you can't get what God wants for you until you go through your passage of pain.

David recorded his passage of pain in Psalm 23. He said, *"Yea though I walk through the valley of the shadow of death, I will not fear."* David was not always on the mountaintop, he had to go through the valley. Even still, David remembered the Lord's provisions, *"Thou preparest a table before me in the presence of mine enemies; thou anointest my head with oil; my cup runneth over."* David took the time to celebrate God's presence while being pursued by his enemies. David completed his famous writing by expressing, *"Surely goodness and mercy shall follow me all the days of my life: and I will dwell in the house of the Lord forever."* As stated earlier, his affection for God's house allowed him the fortitude to fight for God's cause.

Like David, we must go through the passage of pain having an aspiration for the cause of God. This is possible with an ardent desire for the person of Christ, not possessions in life. God will give you possessions, but don't let possessions get you. If you take inventory of your possessions and conclude you have nothing, don't complain. Praise God for nothing, and watch Him give you something. David lost everything and still praised the Lord.

> *Now his elder son was in the field: and as*
> *he came and drew nigh to the house, he*
> *heard musick and dancing. (Luke 15:25)*

Let's revisit Jesus' parable of the man with lost sons. The elder brother was in a terrible condition. Unlike his younger brother he never left his father's house. However, his state was worse because he never had his father's heart. The father celebrated his younger son's return, but the elder brother failed to rejoice. The bible records the older son's reaction to his brother's return as follows, *"And he called one of the servants, and asked what these things meant"* (Lu. 15:26). It's a sad commentary to be in the father's house and ask the meaning of music and dancing.

When you have an aspiration for the cause of God you develop a deep celebratory spirit during times of trouble. The way to break the chains of persecution is by praising the Lord. The word *musick* is *orcho*; it is where we get the English word, orchestra. The Greek word *orcho* connotes, dance with music.

Jesus asked, how is it that when we play celebratory music, nobody dances? When we play somber music, nobody cries? (Matthew 11:17). Dance is a powerful tool. The Native Americans recognized the power of dance. So, they developed a war dance. Dance is a sign language. In order to dance you just have to get your feet off the ground. People know something good has happened or will take place when they see you dance.

Praise is a powerful tool when you have an aspiration for the cause of God. Let's consider praise through metathesis. Metathesis means the changing of letters or syllables in a word that changes the word altogether. The Greek word *orcho* and *choro* share the same meaning. They also share the same letters even though the letters are rearranged. Choro is chorus-meaning singing. Whether we sing, dance or both; we honor God with our praise.

We must maintain an appreciation for God's Word, affection for God's house and keep an aspiration for God's cause. When we operate within these principles we will experience the blessedness of happiness. And, every day in every way we can say—I'm doing better.

CHAPTER NINE REFLECTIONS

_____ is critical in determining how we progress

in life. Success will rise or fall because of _____.

Being blessed is a state of supreme _____.

The world's happiness derives from an old Anglo-Saxon word,

"_____." Happenstance is where we get the

English word "_____."

As Christians, our _____ is rooted in our

relationship with the Lord.

Our blessedness stems from our _____ _____

with God.

We must have an _____ for God's Word, _____

for God's house and an _____ for God's cause.

Appreciation for the Word of God

Jesus Christ is the _____ of God personified.

Jesus is the _____ (Jhn. 14:6). God's Word is the _____

(Jhn. 17:17). Therefore, Jesus and the Word are one in the same.

Our appreciation for the Lord will reflect how we treat His

_____.

As we receive God's _____, _____ and

_____ we will discover good success.

It must be understood that partial obedience is _____.

Sometimes family members and friends suffer because of the

_____ of God's servants.

Respect for God's Word ensures us of His _____

and _____.

It's impossible to have an _____ for God's Word

without having _____ for the Lord's house.

Affection for the House of God

If you love the _____ of the house; then you have to love the

_____ of God.

A sure fire way we display our love for the Lord is how we treat

His _____.

We must come to the house of God with gladness not

_____, or _____, _____

and _____.

You may not always hit the mark or make the right decisions, but

God will _____ you.

In life we will experience hard times, but we can rejoice. Our re-

joicing is not about the _____ in life, but our

_____ in Christ.

Aspiration for the Cause of God

There is a difference between inspiration and _____.

_____ is something you feel on the inside.

_____ is a desire, a longing.

To reach the purpose of God and fulfill His will means going

through _____.

There is no one who lives for God who will not be _____

(2 Tim 3:12).

The way to break the chains of persecution is by _____

the Lord.

We must maintain _____ for God's Word,

_____ for God's house and keep an

_____ for God's cause.

CHAPTER 10

DIVIDING ASUNDER

*For the word of God is quick, and powerful, and sharper than any two-edged sword, piercing even to the **dividing asunder** of soul and spirit, and of the joints and marrow, and is a discerner of the thoughts and intents of the heart.*
(Hebrews 4:12 Bold Added)

MANY PEOPLE HAVE NOT gotten very far in life because they are leaning on someone other than the Lord Jesus. Yet, if we are going to do better, we must lean on Jesus Christ. He is the center and circumference; He's the base and boundary; the balance and beauty; the sum and substance of what our lives are all about. We wouldn't be here if it wasn't for Jesus.

In the beginning was the Word, and the Word was with God, and the Word was God. The same was in the beginning with God. All things were made by him; and without him was not any thing made that was made... And the Word was made flesh, and dwelt among us."(John 1:1-3, 14)

Everything was made by and through Jesus. God knows how we're put together and what's needed to keep us functioning at an optimum level. In fact, we are able to do better through the *"dividing asunder."* The dividing as under is a process performed by the Lord Jesus Christ.

Even if you are under a doctor's care, nobody can treat you like Jesus—the Great Physician. Your physician can treat you with pills and sometimes the pills worsen your condition. Nevertheless, Jesus can take you beyond medicine and perform miracles. He can heal and redeem you. Jesus Christ can make you feel better than any medication the doctor prescribes.

Now, I'm not telling you not to take medication when needed. I am conveying Jesus is the Great Physician. Medication is designed to be digested. Likewise, being divided asunder starts inwardly to produce Christ-like behavior outwardly.

The words *"dividing asunder"* is translated in the Greek as *"merismos."* Merismos is a compound word made up of the words, *"meriso"* and *"meros."*

Meriso means to take apart; separate; divide. A jeweler can take a watch apart piece by piece. That's what Jesus wants to do with us. We are humans. However, we don't know our parts. Jesus is the Merismos Man, meaning He knows every part. He divides asunder the body, soul and spirit.

Nothing man-made can separate the soul from the spirit. Psychiatrists and psychologists come up with ideas and some of them are good, but they cannot separate the soul from the spirit. Nobody but Jesus can accomplish that feat. He divides *"the soul and spirit, joints and marrow, and is a discerner of the thoughts and intents of the heart"* (Heb. 4:12b).

Meros is a division of allotments and shares. It's like when you get your paycheck and your money goes to a division of allotments and shares. A division of your cash goes here, an allotment goes there, and another part may go for something else. This is what *merismos* is all about. Jesus is able to take what's wrong out of us, and put what is right in us.

God wants us to have a forward mind (2 Cor. 9:2). In other words, He wants us to go forward in our minds. So decide today you're not going back or turning back. Stop looking back because what God has for you is forward. Proclaim "I'm doing better, divided asunder by the Lord Jesus Christ."

AN EVIL HEART OF UNBELIEF

So I sware in my wrath, They shall not enter into my rest. Take heed, brethren, lest there be in any of you an evil heart of unbelief, in departing from the living God. (Hebrews 3:11-12)

Something is seriously wrong with people in the world and we need to be delivered. You might ask, "Delivered from whom?" Some people may answer "We need deliverance from the devil." However, we start by being delivered from ourselves. The body craves satisfaction and will sometimes stoop low to get it. For that reason, we need to look at ourselves in the mirror and say, "No," when necessary.

Instead of telling our "self" no, there's a propensity to say "Yes." However, the same way we teach little children discipline, we must undergo our own training. God corrects us in order to keep us safe. Likewise, we should correct ourselves. God gives us what He wants for us not what we want for ourselves. It will take faith to acquire God's will. Many people come short of God's purpose because of unbelief.

God swore the people who operated in unbelief would not experience His rest (Heb. 3:11-12). Notice the Lord did not say "A *wicked* heart of unbelief." He said, "An *evil* heart of unbelief." Evil when spelled backwards is "live." The revelation is simply evil is living without God. There are people who leave God out of their lives. The consequence of a life without God is no rest.

Christians who leave God out the equation of their lives eventually depart from the living God. Rather than removing God from our lives lets follow the scripture that tells us *"Trust in the Lord with all thine heart; and lean not unto thine own understanding. In all thy ways acknowledge him, and he shall direct thy paths"* (Prov. 3:5-6).

Many people are lost because they are directing their own paths. Yet, Jesus is the "way, truth, and life" (Jhn. 14:6). It's important to know Jesus is not *a way*, but He is *The Way*. He's called the "Good Shepherd," the "Great Shepherd" and "Chief Shepherd." The Bible depicts God's people as sheep. Sheep need a shepherd to lead them or they will wander. Even worse, a life of unbelief can cause God's spiritual sheep to abandon the Shepherd.

After review I have discovered there are two types of unbelief. The first type of unbelief is *apistia*, and it means:

1. No faith

2. Lack of faith

3. Little faith

We are told in Hebrews 11:6, *"Without faith it is impossible to please God."* Our goal should be to please Him. So, the question becomes, "How do we get faith? The Word of God reveals, *"So then faith cometh by hearing, and hearing by the word of God"* (Rom. 10:17).

Some people go to church, but they won't hear the Word of God. They'll say, "Well, that's not for me. I'm not going to do what the preacher is saying because I'll live my life my way." These same people are punished because they feel they don't have to listen to the preacher. These rebels need to ask themselves, "Is the Word being preached?" If the answer is "Yes, the Word is going forth," then they should increase in faith. Our faith is increased in two ways:

1. Hearing the Word

2. Obeying the Word

There are people who hear the Word, but they won't obey the Word. This develops an evil heart of unbelief. They choose to do differently because they feel the preacher is tampering with their lifestyle. Yet, when God saves, you are born again; you become a new person. This means, *"Old things are passed away; behold, all things are become new"* (2 Cor. 5:17).

Then there are people who get offended because of the preached Word. And, the offended often take it out on the pastor. Why take it out on the pastor when he's only preaching the Word? If you take it out on the pastor, you are in essence taking it out on the Lord. Now, this is a bad place indeed because nobody can beat God. Your anger will be to no avail and you may find yourself in a humiliating situation.

Jonah received a word from the Lord, but he took offence with the word he heard. Rather than obeying the word, Jonah chose to disobey and go his own way. As punishment, God caused a big fish to swallow Jonah whole.

Amazingly, Jonah survived the fish attack and remained alive in the fish's belly. Even in this horrific condition Jonah wouldn't pray to God. Jonah had an evil heart of unbelief and he wanted to die. Even so, God would not permit death, only suffering. Jonah was in the belly of the fish three days and three nights before finally humbling himself. He prayed and cried for God's mercy. Then God caused the fish to spew Jonah out (Jonah 2).

There are some people who become offended with God's Word and remain that way for three days, weeks, months, maybe even years. Like Jonah, they refuse to seek God's help. However, the Lord knows how to divide asunder. God will punish rebellious people physically in order to save them spiritually.

God wants us all to do better and if that means placing us in the belly of a fish to achieve the results, He will. Even when we disobey God, He is willing to forgive our sins. He extends to anyone who asks His grace and mercy.

⬥ Grace is when God gives you what you don't deserve.

⬥ Mercy is when God withholds what you deserve.

Faith is vital to live the Christian life. Without faith, you're operating in unbelief. Take heed to what befell the children of Israel. Their lack of faith was recorded in the Word of God: *"So we see that they could not enter in because of unbelief."* (Heb. 3:19).

God delivered the children of Israel from Egypt and Pharaoh. Egypt is a type of the world. God brought them out of the world, but they could not go into the Promised Land. So, where were they? They were in the desert for forty years tormented by the devil because of their unbelief (apistia). Collectively they had no faith, a lack of faith, and little faith. If you have little faith, you need to increase it because Christianity is progressive. We should progress from the milk to the meat of God's Word.

A baby is nourished through milk, but the baby matures to meat as he develops. The same holds true for Christians, we have to move from the milk to the meat of God's Word. There are Christians whom God has delivered out of Satan's hands, but they are still living in the wild (wilderness). God will keep them in the wild until they dispel unbelief and develop faith. Only by faith can we enter God's promised life.

Israel's Promised Land flowed with milk and honey. Our promised life possesses prosperity as well. God has new houses, automobiles, and other life amenities. These things are accessible through our obedience to and our faith in the Lord. We are to do better in life by coming out of the wilderness and into God's will.

Again, the first type of unbelief is *apista*. Now, the second type of unbelief is *apeitheia* and it means:

1. Disobedience

2. Rebellion

3. Stubbornness

Some people are in unbelief because they never heard the Word of God. However, there are those people who have heard the truth of God's Word, but are disobedient, rebellious and stubborn.

As we discuss unbelief, consider the following scriptures:

*For unto us was the gospel preached,
as well as unto them: but the word preached
did not profit them, not being mixed with
faith in them that heard it. (Hebrews 4:2)*

*Seeing therefore it remaineth that some
must enter therein, and they to whom
it was first preached entered not in
because of unbelief. (Hebrews 4:6)*

*Let us labour therefore to enter into that
rest, lest any man fall after the same
example of unbelief. (Hebrews 4:11)*

Hebrews chapter four makes a distinct difference between "Us" and "Them." This distinction occurs through the process of diving asunder. The people who were recorded as "Us" operated in faith. On the other hand, the people listed as "Them" lived in a state of unbelief. Now I want to ask, "Are you an 'Us' or 'Them?'" Today, the people in the "Them" category miss God's best; the "Us" individuals receive God's blessings and proclaim, "I'm doing better!"

Nowadays, some of "Them" keep coming to "Us" needing help with paying their rent, car-note or life's other necessities. They always need help because they are not with "Us" and are content to remain with "Them." The "Them" don't receive the faith of God and consequently suffer and struggle on their own.

Yet, God tells "Us" He *will supply all your need according to His riches in glory by Christ Jesus* (Phil. 4:19).

My wife and I know what it is to sleep on the floor. Hardship for us was a norm. Then we placed our faith in the living God and He brought us from poverty to prosperity. The Lord doesn't love one and hate another; He loves us all. Nevertheless, if we don't follow His instructions, we default to the "Them" category. Now, I love "Them." I even help "Them." Yet, I refuse to live like "Them" in unbelief. I will not behave in disobedience, rebellion or stubbornness. I'm going to remain an "Us" on God's side.

GET BACK IN ORDER

God loves order. He is very meticulous in how He goes about His business. He created everything to flow according to their specific systems. That being said, humanity is no exception. Humans are tri-part beings comprised of spirit, soul and body (1 Thess. 5:23). Only when we cultivate all three components are we considered whole.

Some Christians are considered carnal because their soul dominates and dictates their appetite and behavior. When this occurs the Christian is out of order; their system is failing. To get things back in order there must be the dividing asunder of soul and spirit (Heb. 4:12). This means the spirit must come before the soul and the soul before the body.

THE SPIRIT

The Greek word for spirit is *pneuma*. The Apostle Paul said, "I pray God that your whole *spirit* and soul and body be preserved..."(1 Thess. 5:23). See, that's the right order: spirit, soul and body. Now, before salvation we experienced the opposite; it was the body, soul and spirit. In fact, we were spiritually dead—alienated from God. Before we received the Lord's salvation our only concern was the body and soul.

God said, "let us make man in our image, after our likeness:" (Gen. 1:26). God is a Spirit and He also made man a spirit. Afterwards, God blew life into man's nostrils; making him a living soul" (Gen. 2:7). Then God took the dust of the ground and made man a body. Now, the three-part being called man was completed.

> For as many as are led by the Spirit of God,
> they are the sons of God. (Romans 8:14)

We are God's sons when we follow God's Spirit. The term son in this text means mature. Our spirit man desires to grow up in the things of God before we go up to be with the Lord.

THE SOUL

> I am crucified with Christ: nevertheless I live; yet not
> I, but Christ liveth in me: and the life which I now live
> in the flesh I live by the faith of the Son of God, who
> loved me, and gave himself for me. (Galatians 2:20)

Like Paul, we have to learn to crucify the "I." The "I" or ego as it is sometimes referred to loves to be in control. The "I" is our soul. The soul is also considered the flesh. Drop the letter "H" from the word flesh and spell it backwards. The word becomes "self." Self must be crucified.

Again, *"I'm crucified with Christ: nevertheless I live; yet not I, but Christ lives in me"* (Gal. 2:20). The phrase *"Yet not I, but Christ lives in me"* indicates proper order. In essence, the spirit told the soul, "You are out of line; you're not supposed to be in front of me." The spirit must take precedence over the soul.

THE BODY

*But I keep under my body, and bring it into
subjection: lest that by any means, when
I have preached to others, I myself should
be a castaway. (1 Corinthians 9:27)*

The Apostle Paul wrote how he kept his body under, because if he didn't, he would be a castaway. We must discipline our bodies because without constant control these bodies will act contrary to God's will. The human body is not saved. Thus, we must subjugate the body by keeping it under God's influence.

✧ We are saved instantly in the spirit.

✧ We are saved progressively in the soul.

✧ God has another *body* for us.

Maintaining the proper order as you conduct your affairs is paramount. So, feed your spirit with God's Word and a healthy prayer life. Monitor your thought life in order to nurture your soul. Definitely keep control over your body. Decide now you'll allow the Lord to divide you asunder. Then you can proclaim "I'm doing better!"

CHAPTER TEN REFLECTIONS

We are able to do better through the " _dividing_
Assunder ."

Being divided asunder starts _inwardly_ to produce
Christ-like behavior _Outwardly_ .

Jesus is the _Merismos_ Man, meaning He knows every
part. He divides asunder the _body_ , _soul_
and _spirit_ .

God wants us to have a _forward_ mind (2 Cor. 9:2).

An Evil Heart of Unbelief

Many people come short of God's purpose because of _un_
belief .

God swore the people who operated in ~~forward~~ _unbelief_ would
not experience His rest (Heb. 3:11-12). Notice the Lord did not
say "A _wicked_ heart of unbelief." He said, "An _evil_
_____ heart of unbelief." Evil when spelled backwards is
" _live_ ." The revelation is simply evil is living without
God .

It's important to know Jesus is not _a_ way, but He is _The_

Way.

Jesus is called the " _Good_ Shepherd," the " _Great_

Shepherd" and " _Chief_ Shepherd."

The first type of unbelief is _apistia_, and it means:

1. _No faith_
2. _Lack of faith_
3. _Little faith_

Our faith is increased in two ways:

1. _Hearing the Word_
2. _Obeying the Word_

God will punish rebellious people physically in order to save them

spiritually.

Grace is when God gives you what you don't

deserve.

Mercy is when God withholds what you deserve.

Christianity is _progressive_. We should progress from the

milk to the _meat_ of God's Word.

The second type of unbelief is *apeitheia* and it means:

1. _Disobedience_
2. _Rebellion_
3. _Stubbornness_

Get Back in Order

Humans are tri-part beings comprised of _Spirit_,
Soul and _body_ (1 Thess. 5:23).

The Spirit

We are God's sons when we follow God's _Spirit_.
The term son in this text means _mature_.

The Soul

Drop the letter "H" from the word flesh and spell it backwards.
The word becomes "_Self_." Self must be
Crucified.

The Body

The human body is not saved. Thus, we must subjugate the body
by keeping it under _God's_ influence.

DON'T WORRY ABOUT A THING

Be careful for nothing; but in every thing by prayer
and supplication with thanksgiving let your requests
be made known unto God. And the peace of God,
which passeth all understanding, shall keep your
hearts and minds through Christ Jesus.
(Philippians 4:6-7 KJV)

IT IS MY SINCERE DESIRE for you to do better. More importantly, God created you for the purpose of doing better. In the beginning, God created man to have dominion, to multiply and increase while subduing the earth. In a nutshell, "Do better!"

The Lord wants you rooted and grounded in Him. His desire is that you comprehend the breadth, length, depth and height of His love. Then, you will have the capability of receiving God's fullness (Eph. 3:17-19).

When we are filled with all the fullness of God, we can attack hell with an empty water pistol and the fire will be out before we get there. The Bible tells us, "Be careful for nothing; but in everything by prayer and supplication with thanksgiving let your requests be made known unto God. And the peace of God, which passes all understanding, shall keep your hearts and minds through Christ Jesus" (Philippians 4:6-7).

"Be careful for nothing" means "Don't worry about a thing." God does not want us worrying about anything. Without the Lord we have every reason in this world to worry. This world is filled with all sorts of trouble because of the devil's plots, ploys, and plans. Satan's agenda is to steal, kill and to destroy (John 10:10). He is the one who brings problems, pain and pressure. Regardless, God has written, "Be careful for nothing."

CHOOSE CONTENTMENT
NOT CARE

God wants us to learn to live with contentment because it strangles any care we may have. When the Apostle Paul said, "Be careful for nothing" he was conveying rest with peace because God is going to take care of us. The word care is the Greek word *merimna*. *Merimna* carries the connotation of an uneasy, fearful feeling about the outcome. Fearing the outcome eventually leads to the sin of worry. Be careful for nothing is not a suggestion, it's a command. And, ensconced in every command is the promise of victory. When we step out and obey God's command we will experience good success.

> *Humble yourselves therefore under the mighty hand of God, that he may exalt you in due time: Casting all your care upon him; for he careth for you.* (1 Peter 5:6-7)

God doesn't want us filled with anxieties, worries or fears about anything. He is a supernatural God. People often say, "I'm going to let God handle the big stuff and I'll take care of the little stuff." But they fail to realize it's all little to God. The Lord is large and in charge and everything we face is smaller than Him. He does not want us worried about anything.

So how do we keep from worrying? I'm glad you asked. We must keep our minds on the Lord. Whenever you face a dilemma you can say, "God you have a problem." God says, "Be careful for nothing; but in everything by prayer and supplication with thanksgiving let your requests be made known unto Him." Authentic prayer displays faith in God. God will take care of us if we obey Him. God will supply all our need according to His riches in glory by Christ Jesus (Phil. 4:19).

Nowadays the mainstream philosophy is, "Be self-made." If you made yourself then you worship yourself, however, you can't take care of yourself. God did not create man to live in this world without Him. We need God. Without Him the devil will torment us with worry. Worry causes us to torment ourselves with disturbing thoughts. In essence we are saying, "I don't believe God can do what He said He would do." This is not good. So, choose contentment not care.

We must learn contentment in God and with Him. Contentment is an uncomplaining acceptance of one's lot in life. Many people think a certain position will make them content, but they are mistaken. If you are not content where you are, there will be no contentment when you arrive at your destination. God's preparing us for what He has prepared for us. If we're discontent, we will stumble, fumble and crumble under the weight of adversity. God wants us to grow up before we go up.

David was content. Even as a young man he did not complain about his life. He did not ask for a life of royalty. Yet, the Lord sent Samuel the prophet to pull him from the background to the forefront. God chose David to be king.

When Samuel arrived at Jesse's house all but *one* of Jesse's sons were brought before the prophet. None of the men who were presented qualified for the king's position. While all of Jesse's sons were filled with care concerning their possible promotion, David contentedly worked in the fields. Samuel denied all of Jesse's sons—well, all who were presented to him. The only son left out of the line-up was David, the youngest.

Many people think Jesse failed to present David because of

his youthfulness. Personally, I believe Jesse preferred Samuel take any of his sons with the exception of David. David's contented disposition made him a valued asset. Quite possibly his contentment made him a man after God's own heart (Acts 13:22).

Some people complain about everything. Their discontentment stems from disbelief in God's ability to fix their problem. God lifts and helps when we humble ourselves under His mighty hand (James 4:10). Many times we try to figure out what only God can work out. God sees everything and He knows how and what He is going to do. The Lord is admonishing us not to worry about a thing; and to learn contentment. Learn to have a restful, peaceful state of mind, knowing that God is taking care of us. David chose not to care, but to remain content. And, from his perspective he announced, "The LORD is my shepherd; I shall not want" (Psalm 23:1).

God will make us lie down because He cares for us. He doesn't want us to breakdown or be torn down. God makes a way where there is no way. Do we believe God or not? Who hath believed God's report and to whom is the arm of the LORD revealed?" (Isa. 53:1). Contentment is developed by believing the report of the Lord. David said of God, "You prepare a table before me in the presence of my enemies" (Psalm 23:5a). God used David's enemies, not his friends, to feed him in the wilderness and He'll do the same for us. So choose contentment not care.

RECEIVE GOD'S REST
AND CHRIST'S LIFE

Come unto me, all ye that labour and are
heavy laden, and I will give you rest. Take
my yoke upon you, and learn of me; for I am
meek and lowly in heart: and ye shall find
rest unto your souls. For my yoke is easy, and
my burden is light. (Matthew 11:28-30)

If you are carrying a heavy load, Jesus wants you to receive His rest. God is the only one who can give us rest from stress, struggle and strain. He tells us, "Take my yoke upon you." Receiving the Lord's rest means we become workers together with Him.

A good farmer does not put two strong oxen together, because they will fight against each other. Instead the farmer pairs a strong ox with a weak ox; the strong ox carries the mother-load. The weaker or younger ox is learning how to carry the load. This is what Jesus is saying to us, "Take my yoke upon you, and learn of me" (Matt. 11:29). When we learn of Him, we learn we can rest in Him.

Consider the following scriptures:

And the peace of God, which passeth all
understanding, shall keep your hearts and
minds through Christ Jesus. (Philippians 4:7)

*Those things, which ye have both learned, and
received, and heard, and seen in me, do: and the
God of peace shall be with you. (Philippians 4:9)*

*Now the Lord of peace himself give you
peace always by all means. The Lord be
with you all. (2 Thessalonians 3:16)*

*Let your conversation be without covetousness;
and be content with such things as ye
have: for he hath said, I will never leave
thee, nor forsake thee. (Hebrews 13:5)*

The overarching theme in all the previous scriptures is we have God's presence so we can rest with peace. Peace is not the absence or dismissal of your problems, pain or pressure. Peace is an acknowledgment and admission of the Lord's presence, power and promises.

*Let your conversation be without covetousness;
and be content with such things as ye
have: for he hath said, I will never leave
thee, nor forsake thee. (Hebrews 13:5)*

The Greek word for conversation is *tropos*, which is the way you live your life. God says, "Let your conversation [the way you live your life] be without covetousness [desiring what someone else has]." Then He says, "Be content with such things as ye have: for he hath said, I will never leave thee, nor forsake thee."

Being content with the things you have means resting in the Lord. No matter what you have or where you are, rest knowing God is present. He will never leave you spiritually or abandon you emotionally. Remember, the Lord is your helper, and you need not fear what the adversary can do to you (Heb. 13:5b-6). Meditate and think on that promise and it will dissolve any kind of worry the devil tries to bring. God doesn't want us to worry about a thing. He wants us to learn to be content and have rest and peace in Him.

> For whatsoever is born of God overcometh the
> world: and this is the victory that overcometh
> the world, even our faith. (1 John 5:4)

In order for us to overcome some things we must go through some things. The Bible says, "Remember them which have the rule over you, who have spoken unto you the word of God: whose faith follow, considering the end of their conversation" (Hebrews 13:7). Conversation used in this verse is the Greek word *anastrophe* which is how we live the Christ life.

God does not want us living our lives the way we lived without Him. Many people keep on living "their life" after they get "His Life." God is saying, "Live the Christ life." Listen to the following words of our Lord, "I am the good shepherd: the good shepherd giveth his life for the sheep." "I am come that they might have life, and that they might have it more abundantly" (John 10:10-11).

By living the Christ Life our moderation will be known (Philippians 4:5). The word moderation is connected to contentment and it's the evidence we have received Jesus' rest. Through moderation we allow our rest and peaceful state of mind to be known to all men.

When I first received salvation I went home and flushed all my drugs down the toilet. My friends came by and asked, "Where is the stuff?" I said, "I flushed that stuff down the toilet." They said, "Why would you do something like that?" I said, "Man, I'm saved now." You can simply tell people, "I'm saved," or you can show them by living the Christ Life.

"Let your moderation be known unto all men. The Lord is at hand" (Philippians 4:5). Let people know Jesus Christ is Lord by the way you live your life. Knowing the Lord is at hand gives us God's peace allowing us to rest. When this occurs we won't worry about a thing.

DON'T CHOOSE FEAR USE FAITH

. . .for he hath said, I will never leave thee, nor forsake thee. So that we may boldly say, The Lord is my helper, and I will not fear what man shall do unto me. (Hebrews 13:5-6 KJV)

The writer of this passage understood three very important things. First, God will never leave us. Second, the Lord is our helper. Finally, we need not fear whatever men devise against us. Rather than choosing fear we can use faith.

The Bible tells of a woman who was stricken with pain. In the span of twelve years this woman suffered with severe hemorrhaging. Because of this issue she was isolated from family and friends; as a recluse, she craved relief.

Her money was squandered on medical treatment that never produced the cure; her hopes of recovery tattered from one broken promise to the next. She was disconnected and rejected by the community at large.

One day she received word of a man who worked wonders, a healer who helped. Someone told her about Jesus and His power to deliver the bruised, battered, and broken. Then she yearned the day for a chance encounter with this Miracle Man whose knack was changing negatives into positives.

Unannounced, Jesus came in close proximity of this woman. Her thoughts erupted like a Roman candle, "Can He heal me? Will He heal me?" Finally she decided to approach Him. However, there was one major problem. A great crowd of people stood between this woman's hurt and the Healer.

Jesus was surrounded by a mob that grew larger by the minute. By law this woman's physical condition disallowed her public appearance. In fact, to be seen in public could have meant death. Although this woman faced a great dilemma, she pressed through the hostile crowd.

Her help was within arm's reach; her deliverance within earshot. The only thing that stood between her and Jesus was the crazed crowd. She was forced to choose between playing it safe or risking it all.

Fortunately, she chose to move beyond her fear and utilize her faith. She exchanged her issue for Jesus' virtue. Because she dared touch God He in turn touched her.

Beloved, understand God is the CEO of the universe. Nothing happens concerning your life without first clearing His desk and receiving His approval.

Mary the mother of Jesus was the coordinator of a wedding reception. The ceremony went smooth as the couple exchanged their vows. We can safely assume this because the Bible mentions nothing about the couple's nuptials. The families of the bride and groom were there in full support. This couple could have held some social status because the governor showed up to endorse the event himself.

Everything during the day went according to plan. Now, everyone sought to unwind and they did until the party had no wine. The servants reached a point of panic then they looked to Mary for pointers. As the coordinator, Mary's reputation could have been ruined. However, rather than choosing fear, she utilized her faith in Jesus.

In essence, Mary's demeanor conveyed, "Don't worry about a thing." While the servants thoughts went to the family, wedding party and esteemed honored guests, Mary thought of one person—Jesus. Mary directed the workers to Jesus because she knew He was a trouble shooter. Mary gave her employees one specific instruction which was, "What He [Jesus] says—do it!" (Jhn. 2:5).

Jesus told the servants to fill pots with water and serve it first to the governor. When they obeyed Jesus and served the official, the governor tasted the water-turned-wine and shared his extreme pleasure with the entire room. Scientists might consider this account a lab experiment, but the wedding participants were not given a placebo, they were handed a miracle.

When we trust God and obey His Word in spite of how the situation appears, we receive the best results. In every scenario choose to be content. Model the life of Christ. And, never choose fear when you have the option to optimize your faith in God. If you can follow these instructions you will no doubt be able to say, "I'm doing better."

CHAPTER 11 REFLECTIONS

The Lord wants you <u>rooted</u> and <u>grounded</u> in His love.

"Be careful for nothing" means "<u>Don't worry about a thing</u>."

Satan's agenda is to <u>Steal</u>, <u>kill</u> and to <u>destroy</u> (John 10:10).

Choose Contentment Not Care

God wants us to learn to live with <u>Contentment</u> because this strangles any care we may have.

Fearing the outcome eventually leads to the sin of <u>worry</u>.

Be careful for nothing is not a suggestion, it's a <u>command</u>.

Authentic prayer is faith in <u>God</u>.

Worry causes us to <u>torment</u> ourselves with disturbing thoughts.

<u>Contentment</u> is an uncomplaining acceptance of one's lot in life.

If we're ___discontent___, we will stumble, fumble and crumble under the weight of the adversary.

Contentment develops by believing the ___report___ of the Lord.

Receive God's Rest and Christ's Life

God is the only one who can give us rest from ___stress___, ___struggle___ and ___strain___.

Receiving the Lord's rest means we become ___workers___ together with Him.

FEAR IS A THIEF AND A ROBBER

...taking by stealth and by force one of your most priceless commodities: confidence. In fact, fear is faith perverted and misplaced. Though governed by the same principles, faith's confidence rests in God, while fear trusts in the inevitability of the worst possible outcome. But you can be delivered from all your fears.

Your journey through this book will teach you how to obliterate the fears that have long plagued you—facing them, tracing them, erasing them, and replacing them with faith. When faith is present, fear is powerless and confidence is at optimum levels. **So let's begin this journey toward an unrestricted life, filled with potential, unabated by fear.**

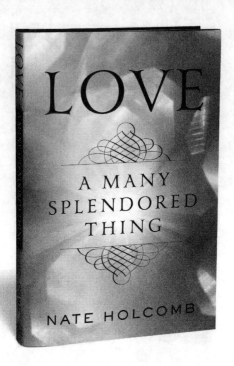

LEARN TO LIVE WITH PURPOSE

The Purpose of Living transcends personal vocation and ventures into the impact on the very essence of life itself. To find *The Purpose of Living* elevates the stature and station of a person's life because he or she lays hold of a key which, once turned, unlocks principles conducive to nothing but provision, promotion, and prosperity in every aspect of life. In this book Nate Holcomb teaches that glorifying God with your time, talents, gifts, possessions, and money is a form of economics. God has sown these things in you; and in serving Him with them, you're giving Him a return with interest on His investment.

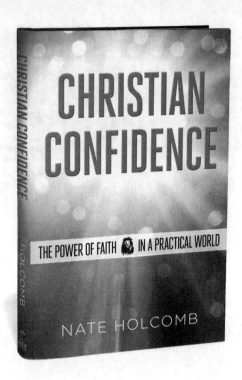

LIFE'S HARD-KNOCKS HAVE LEFT MANY DESTITUTE AND DREAMLESS, *BUT THAT DOES NOT HAVE TO BE THE END*

Nate Holcomb explores the concept of a life lived to the fullest. He details how God created mankind for progress and advancement, despite conflicting internal and external forces. He discloses the Laws of Progress which transcend any obstacles, and introduces the next dimension of faith; where one comes to know God through experience— *Christian Confidence.*

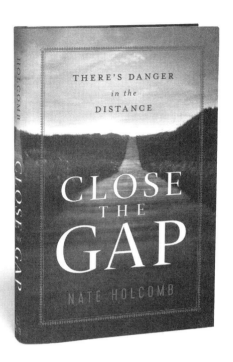

FOLLOWING FROM AFAR PUTS US AT A DISADVANTAGE

The Lord commanded Peter twice in John chapter 21 to "Follow me." He was telling Peter to start where he was, leave fishing, and assume the position of a disciple that attends to the matters of the Lord. Perhaps you find yourself in Peter's position; you are following the Lord from afar. Beloved, just as it was with Peter, the Lord is calling you unto Himself. He's beckoning you to come in close proximity. He's telling you to assume the position of a follower, and to follow hard upon His heels until you arrive at your destination. So, *close the gap!*

Grow Up Before You Go Up

CHRISTIAN MATURITY

NATE HOLCOMB

Spiritual Principles to Take You from Milk to Meat

Using divine building blocks such as confession, meditation and spiritual confidence, you will be able to wean yourself from man-made formulas. You will draw sustenance from the strong meat of the word that builds spiritual stamina and maturity, while fortifying godly character.

In *Christian Maturity*, you will learn how to wean yourself from impeding habits, while developing a regimen that stimulates personal growth.